"Glorious . . . A work that breaks the mold."
—*People*

"Hilarious and horny, but also poignant and
tender . . . Slate has an inimitable voice,
which is one that, once you've heard it,
you want to listen to forever."
— *Nylon*

"The 'weirds' may be little, but the
themes and feelings arc huge."
—*Teen Vogue*

"As charmingly disarming as any of
the actress's on-screen work."
—*Entertainment Weekly*

"Completely unlike anything you've ever read."
— *San Francisco Book Review*

"*Little Weirds* is a fairy tale, one where the prince
is never all charming, where your home is never
quite safe, and where you probably won't live
happily ever after. But you will live, and it's
pretty incredible just to do that."
—John Mulaney

"Indescribable...performance art in high-caliber prose." — *Washington Post*

Praise for Jenny Slate's
Little Weirds

A *Vulture* Best Comedy Book of the Year
A *She Reads* Best Celebrity Memoir of the Year
A *Vanity Fair* Great Quarantine Read
A *Marie Claire* Book Club Selection

"At once warm, heartbreaking, and erotic...The essays are unclassifiable...A strange, witty, sad journey into the depths of their author's imagination...Devastating in their unfiltered honesty, even optimism...showcasing Slate's singular poetic forms of expression."
—David Canfield, *Entertainment Weekly*

"Jenny's writing is magical and stylish, just like her. Each essay in *Little Weirds* feels like a vivid, cinematic experience, full of original observations and unexpected laughs."
—Mindy Kaling

"This book is something new and wonderful—honest, funny, positive, completely original, and inspiring in the very best way: it made me remember I was alive."
—George Saunders

"Funny and strange and full of moments of reckoning with loss." —Audie Cornish, NPR's *All Things Considered*

"Luminous, emotional, lovely, and a little mysterious, this book is something you will savor like a half-remembered, gorgeous dream. You'll finish it feeling like Jenny Slate is your new best friend." —Susan Orlean, author of *The Library Book* and *The Orchid Thief*

"Jenny Slate is an artist in the broadest sense of the word...Adjust your expectation of a run-of-the-mill memoir and ready yourself to drop straight into Slate's imagination. Her ability to paint a meticulous mental picture with nothing but words on a page can only be described as gifted." —Associated Press

"A man on the number 2 express train read some of *Little Weirds* over my shoulder. 'What kind of a book is this?' he asked. 'The best kind,' I replied." —John Mulaney

"This book is like a stovetop goulash: delicious and varied ingredients, prepared perfectly and excellent with bread...I'm sorry, I lost track of the simile." —Amy Sedaris

"Jenny's writing is wide open, tuneful, tender. She sees the world (and feels the world) like a bug might, two antennae poking out from her head like sensory wands. Reading *Little Weirds* made me feel tipsy."

—Durga Chew-Bose, author of
Too Much and Not the Mood

"Indescribable but eminently readable... *Little Weirds* is performance art in high-caliber prose."

—Bethanne Patrick, *Washington Post*

"Jenny Slate, the polymathic actress, writer, and comic, presents a delightfully odd assemblage of vignettes whose magical-realist absurdity is a style all her own."

—Drew Tewksbury, *Los Angeles Times*

"A poetic and dreamlike book, a testament to the power of fantasy and language to hit your feelings where facts and pictures can't... The 'weirds' may be little, but the themes and feelings are huge. Because above all, *Little Weirds* is a book about the hazards of love. Loving love, the feeling of it, being burned by it... It's also about the indignities of being a woman... Through it all, Slate's voice never loses its capacity for strangeness, for finding it in the littlest, weirdest corners. And it's this mix of sweet and sadness, real stakes and dreamy prose, that gives this book its soft, sharp, and altogether overwhelming power. Like René Magritte crossed with Lana Del Rey, with strong notes of Patricia Lockwood. Like a carnival ride caught in a tornado, candy-colored shards of metal sparkling in the sky."   —Dennis Tang, *Teen Vogue*

"Reading Jenny Slate's *Little Weirds* is like digesting Shakespearean sonnets: A dreamy dessert for the eyeballs that uses playful language to express deep sentiments about heartbreak, anger, wonder, and friendship."
                                    —Carly Mallenbaum, *USA Today*

"The mind that made you fall in love with a tiny shell hang gliding on a Dorito does similarly strange, albeit more grown-up work in this collection of essays, which touches on everything from haunted houses to a vagina singing sad old songs."   —Samantha Rollins, *Bustle*

"A delight to read. It's a collection of beautiful, hilarious, genuine essays and really is meant for times when you feel heavy. Slate jumps between deeply considering a dead deer on her parents' property, to transcribing her borderline surrealist dreams, to poignantly investigating heartache and the forms it takes, in such a genuine way

I couldn't help but feel that it was written by a friend for me." —Allison Schaller, *Vanity Fair*

"Slate got what most major comedians get—a book deal—and the result is wholly original and uniquely hers…She writes in this lyrical, musical, even poetic way. The guardedness typical of the comedian memoir is thus gloriously stripped away, as is the self-deprecation usually found in such books. Jenny celebrates herself, and her whole being. She manages to be whimsical but hilarious but vulnerable." —Brian Boone, *Vulture*

"*Little Weirds* is hard to classify: it's equal parts memoir and essays, and also what Slate describes as little prayers to herself. It is nonetheless a deep dive into her own interiority—the source of her creativity and pain. Although we can sometimes be the sum of our own destructive thoughts, in *Little Weirds,* there are small creeds and lessons that force you to look at their sources: the narratives we attach to ourselves, the bad patterns they enable, and the triggers that reinforce those patterns." —Sara Black McCulloch, *The Believer*

"Full of soft and lovely moments…Slate beautifully evokes the pleasures of female friendship."—Lily Meyer, NPR.org

"Slate's voice remains an eccentric and powerful central force as she comments on politics, patriarchy, and her personal life."   —Annabel Gutterman, *Time*

"Every so often, someone will decide to stray from the outline and gift us with something so unexpected that it might not tickle our funny bone, but it might tickle us pink. Jenny Slate's nonfiction collection *Little Weirds* is one such book. It's an extremely personal narrative, and there are elements of humor in it, but that may be all it has in common with the efforts of her peers...A collection that relies so heavily on whimsy shouldn't be this effective, but the emotions in it are so raw that delving into her words creates an intimate connection to the work."

—Ines Bellina, *AV Club*

"Rooted in Slate's commitment to beauty and sweetness, as well as her refusal to treat her sorrow as unsightly... Earnest, funny, and effervescent."   —Elahe Izadi, *Washington Post*

"*Little Weirds* explores the oddities—and magic—of everyday life...Together, the entries illustrate how Slate navigates the world, illuminating the oddities of social constructs. Many of the Weirds find Slate in flux, when she discovers the bright side of tough situations and refuses to apologize for her broad spectrum of feelings... *Little Weirds* chattily chronicles Slate's highs and lows and dips and swoops as if the actress is absorbing sunshine through an IV." —Kate Dwyer, *Marie Claire*

"If you weren't previously aware of Slate's dexterity as a storyteller, *Little Weirds* will be your awakening...The thing about Jenny Slate is that her warmth doesn't come just from her openness. It also comes from her ability to say, with her whole chest, something others would keep hushed away...When too many of us have been conditioned to believe it's uncool to care, Slate basks in her unabashed vulnerability. When you're in her presence, whether it be through her writing, her stand-up, or FaceTime, it feels like stepping into a world that has been recalibrated toward more tenderness, more generosity." —Kimberly Truong, *InStyle*

"It has the poignancy of Marcel the Shell but is also very personal and funny and peculiar. It's like nothing you've read. You'll want to sit with the words."—Todd Oldham

"Judging from the content of Jenny Slate's *Little Weirds,* the inside of her mind is a fascinating, if

unusual, place. In this collage of essays, stories, dreams (both night and day), and pieces that defy easy categorization, the actor and comedian invites readers to pay an extended visit, one that will leave them enlightened, moved, and sometimes pleasantly puzzled...This collection promises a refreshing, original journey."
—Harvey Freedenberg, *Shelf Awareness* (starred review)

"There are very few passages in *Little Weirds* that aren't completely unlike anything you've ever read. Slate explores her own psyche in a fascinating way, making readers willing voyeurs...*Little Weirds* is a work of creative nonfiction designed to have readers laughing through their tears while looking deeper into themselves and how they relate to others." —Daniel Casey, *San Francisco Book Review*

"A collection of not quite stories and not quite essays that are somehow more than both...Holding the book together is Slate's intelligence and eye for the absurd, which is to say her voice...Pure joy for her subtlety, sensitivity, and comic timing...Few books explore self-doubt and loneliness with as much fun or creativity...Jenny Slate is very much a writer." —James Tate Hill, *Literary Hub*

Little Weirds

Jenny Slate

Back Bay Books
Little, Brown and Company
New York   Boston   London

Back Bay Books / Little, Brown and Company
Hachette Book Group
1290 Avenue of the Americas, New York, NY 10104
littlebrown.com

Originally published in hardcover by Little, Brown and Company, November 2019

First Back Bay trade paperback edition, November 2020

Back Bay Books is an imprint of Little, Brown and Company, a division of Hachette Book Group, Inc. The Back Bay Books name and logo are trademarks of Hachette Book Group, Inc.

The publisher is not responsible for websites (or their content) that are not owned by the publisher.

The Hachette Speakers Bureau provides a wide range of authors for speaking events. To find out more, go to hachettespeakersbureau.com or call (866) 376-6591.

"The Layers" copyright © 1978 by Stanley Kunitz, from *Passing Through: The Later Poems, New and Selected,* by Stanley Kunitz. Used by permission of W. W. Norton & Company, Inc.

ISBN 978-0-316-48534-0 (hc) / 978-0-316-48536-4 (pb)
LCCN 2019933749

10 9 8 7 6 5 4 3 2 1

LSC-C

Printed in the United States of America

This book is dedicated to my mother,
who is always kind even when
incredibly stubborn.

This book is dedicated to my sisters,
who are two halves of the sun that
warms me.

This book is dedicated to my father, who
is a gift from the universe and an actual
genius, and without whom this book
would not even exist at all.

And this book is dedicated to Quinn,
who is my heart's little mother and the
dearest friend of my truest self.

Contents

Contents

Contents

In the middle of the pouring rain she met (explosion) the first thing she could call a boyfriend in her life, her heart beating as if she'd swallowed a little fluttering and captured bird.

—Clarice Lispector, *The Hour of the Star*

In my darkest night,
when the moon was covered
and I roamed through wreckage,
a nimbus-clouded voice
directed me:
"Live in the layers,
not on the litter."

—Stanley Kunitz, "The Layers"

Little Weirds

Treat

One of my fantasy dimensions is: Strangers on the street see me and think I might be French. You are a stranger. You see me, and you think that there I am, a French Woman. And then you look at me and allow a deeper kind of feeling-sight to occur, and you see past the woman and you sense that I am actually a homemade Parisian Croissant, and I was born in a kitchen in a house with cool stone floors and deep windowsills that hold the light in the shape of a big box, windowsills that are so deep that they could be a desk. I was born as a breakfast pastry in the fancy part of France and hours after I was born I was still warm from the heat of the oven. I knew that my warmth and lovely shape were the result of thoughtful and gentle work. Oh please feel it: I am the croissant that felt its own heat and curves and wished to become a woman, and I am that woman from the wish. Let me be your morning treat with your coffee. Disregard the fear that I am too rich to be an ordinary meal. Allow my antique decadence into your morning into your mouth. Pair me with jam. Treasure me for my layers and layers of fragility and richness. Name me after a shape that the moon makes. Have me in a hotel while you are on vacation. Look at me and say, "Oh, I really shouldn't," just because you want to have me so very much.

There are so many times when I want to be here just for your consumption, just to satisfy your appetite. This is what I feel I am intended for—I can't help it. An intention was inside of me already when I traveled from infinity to a kitchen with a windowsill, to a wish, to a woman.

Introduction/Explanation/Guidelines
for Consumption

Hello, do you have expectations about how we should proceed together? We both know quite well that it is risky to reveal oneself, but I am compelled to do it.

Some time ago, I made peace with wanting to be looked at. There's no secret fold within my feeling, no pleat where I force myself to stow a slip of paper that says "shame" on one side and "weakness" on another (both sides scrawled in haughty cursive by the schoolmistress in my psyche who drinks scalding brown tea). I am fine about having the need.

* * *

I know that to be seen is to be taken in. My delight, this inclination to sweep into your eyesight, beats in me like an extra heart. It just might bat an eyelash at you. My need to be seen is feather-light and active, with a tongue that licks its lips like a mouse peering out of a teacup, looking at the cheese. My need is a helium-filled balloon that wants to be untethered. What is this spirit in me saying "Up! Up! UP!"? Up for a better view, for a better location to be viewed. Get me to a better place so that I can see more and also be spotted by the kind of people who turn their faces up to the light. Put me in between them and the cosmos, let me be one final stop before the major everything.

And actually, there is more about me that is like a balloon.

Hello, I am a balloon on a string that has been tied to this page to announce, "Party here!"

Tie me to the mailbox to mark the place on the dirt road where everyone must bang a left and drive toward a gathering of dressed-up friends. Let the motion of people attracted to this spot kick up soft brown dust as they accelerate toward the final destination, which is *party time*.

About your hostess: I am a human woman named Jenny Slate and I am thirty-boink years old. I weigh one hundred and doo-dad pounds. I was born in Massachusetts as a one-second-old hospital baby. I love eating cucumbers and I love the xylophone and the Atlantic Ocean and I am a performer by nature and trade.

That's enough to form a small shape, like a gal-sized gate, into the rest. Here is more of the rest:

When I am on stage, it is mostly my party. But I am hoping to throw it for us, to honor our having the faith to come together and feel something bubbly and balmy as a collective. I am throwing the party for the sake of itself, for your self, and for my self.

On the stage, I am thrilled and moved. But before being seen by you, I have been terrified, often ill-tempered. I have most likely ruined an entire day by fretting about this evening. Just before I open my mouth on the stage (with bright faith in everything—me, you, that the building won't fall down, that I will catch on to the thing that helps me zoom, that a man won't come in and shoot me, etc.), I have most likely used my same mouth and voice to tell everyone backstage, "I know I say this every time, but I feel really off today. I can tell that it's going to be bad."

Once I'm up there, so many feelings happen at once.

The lights are shining right into my face, so I can't really see you; I imagine you as one complex but benevolent identity. I am nervous but also excited for you to see my onstage outfit chosen just for you and the people. It took many tries to choose this one outfit. I was trying to figure out what I want to be wearing when we all fall in love. On stage and everywhere else, I know that there is so much you could do to me. My vulnerability is natural and permissible and beautiful to me, and it should remind you of your responsibility to behave like a friend to me and the world.

I'm setting the tone and the tone is this: There is a free, wild creature up here, and now you must think about how to take her in and keep her alive. This is the tone that is rippling through the pages up ahead.

* * *

Just as I get scared to perform, I am afraid to write this book. Across the board, I just get so scared. But I don't want to live in a constant state of trepidation. I want to live in front of you, with you. I tremble myself to pieces when I perform. I also put myself back together and I leave without a limp.

Recently my life fell to pieces. These things happened: Pummeling heartbreak. The sickening experience of watching a racist, homophobic, misogynist bully sit right down in the Oval Office. Loss of confidence. Astounding loneliness. Disempowerment and exhaustion.

This book is the act of pressing onward through an inner world that was dark and dismantled.

This book is me putting myself back together so that I can dwell happily in our shared outer world.

Look! Look at this woman who is both the emergency and the relief. Let me be both (I have no choice). Give in. Fall apart. Look at the pieces. Reassemble. This is the essential movement of my holy flux.

* * *

This book is a party—not a set of grievances. It's a weird party for a woman who has returned from grief. It's a peppy procession of all of my little weirds. Many different scenarios present themselves at a really good party. Somebody kisses somebody. Somebody falls. Cake is eaten. Cake is thrown. The lights go out and somebody screams, "My jewels!" You meet your husband for the first time. Somebody gets kicked out. There are snowballs and cannonballs. There are fragments that come together as a whole. My book is a thing in motion—just as you would respond to the question "Is there a party going on?" with the answer "Yes, it is in progress!"

Here it is, a book that represents the wholeness that I built after everything toppled. A book that honors my fragmentation by giving itself to you in pieces. If you want it, you will have to be my partner in giving in to what it is. I had to find my own language and terms.

I am here not just to give myself an opening, not just to direct your view toward an opening, not just to fling you and myself through a density of experience, but, selfishly, so that I can experience the pleasure and honor of hosting you in my private space. It is not a mad or haunted house. But maybe a witch does live here. I am your witch and I nudge the dark waves and I cast the gentle light over the hard terrain. I coax the crocus to open in the frost. I keep the faith and I use it.

My father says, "After a while you understand that you can create and raise the child, but the spirit…the spirit comes from the universe."

You have my permission to come into this space that is made out of broken-up pieces, of shards and perfect circles, slats and slices. It represents the space that I have found to house my spirit, which is from the universe. I was born to host this party. To be in the party, remind you of the party, live at the event, die at the event.

It will be a wild ride, but the fresh air and interesting company are worth all of the frightful bouncing, I believe.

I Was Born: The List

The first thing that happened was that I was born.

And now that I'm shaking out the truth from myself, let's just shake it out for one big shake:

I was born during the great Potato Chip, in the time of Jewish Deli Tongue Sandwich. I was born and the other items that were in the love net in which they caught me were Open Car Windows, Ghosts, Fear, Horniness, Rabbit Holes, Bird Nests, Emily Dickinson, Petticoats, Bustiers, Grapefruit Halves with Maraschino Cherry in the Middle, Chapter Books, Secret Passages, *Sesame Street, Mermaids* starring Cher, a messy bookstore called New England Mobile Book Fair, Grandparents, Ham for Lunch, Gems, Treehouses, Annie Oakley, Chicken Noodle Soup, Crystal Gayle, *Meet Me in St. Louis,* A Stage, A Theater, A Camera, A Bra, A Slip, A Mouth, A Butt and Vagina, Beer, Clarice Lispector, A Beech Tree, A Campfire, Romance, Music, Loneliness.

I was born with a love of dressing up and facing this world with an ecstatic and elegant personal style. I was born as a good girl with the kicky ability to skip so much class that I must owe someone (my grandmother) money for the huge bulk of time that they paid for me to be there and I just simply did not show up because I hate sitting still even when I love the thing that I am sitting to see. I was born with the talent for fucking off so majorly. I was born bucking the idea that I should have to be anywhere that I don't like or talk to people who make me feel dead or trapped.

I was born into a world where many men want to oppress all of the women with violence and laws and you or I can't say anything else anymore without also admitting that.

* * *

I was born hating how boring Hebrew School is and how breath is really bad in temple, especially on the day that you are fasting and saying sorry for the entire day. It is so hard because I was born with a love of useful rules but also somehow I am always dropping and breaking them and it makes me feel very bad.

I was born with a love of dogs and a fear of horses and I don't want to change the way I feel about either of these things. I was born in a hatbox on a train in the past, when there were dining cars and menus and bud vases and chaperones and dandies. I was born as sweet as that and if I am too sweet for your tastes then just clamp your mouth shut and spin on your heels. I can't add sourness to my sap anymore just to fit onto a menu in a restaurant for wimps.

I was born in the stacks in the Columbia University Library. I was born in shin-guards on a soccer field on a chilly little Saturday morning in the 1980s and I was too scared to even feel the sting of the ball on the inside of my shoe. I was born during tennis. I was born as a backyard swimming pool and my twin sister is an orange Popsicle and my mother is a bowl of pickles and my father is a hamburger.

* * *

I was born with a ticking clock inside of me that chirped and rang out many years later and its gears lowered my mouth open for a French kiss and made my skirt light up like a lamp with a shade saying "Someone's awake in here…come see who it is."

I was born in a Shirley Temple, and I came out with the stem of the cherry in my small, strong new hand and I walked that cherry like a dog. I was born ready to care for a pet and be a pet too.

I was born like that.

I was born happy but when anything that is large, alive, and wild gets hurt and confused, I feel so sad, and I notice that I wish I could nurse big scared things. And it is worth mentioning that "big scared thing" is one way to describe how my heart often feels. My heart can feel like an elephant who is feeling dread and has an exceptional memory and naturally possesses something valuable that might be hunted, poached, wasted.

I was born in the Atlantic Ocean, and I pray to goddesses that look like whales and waves and I make tons of wishes. I was born in the day, right before lunchtime, and I arrived with a full appetite and it hasn't settled down at all.

I was born with a fatal allergy to both subtext and traditional organization techniques and I will tell you I have really had a few near-death experiences. I was born two years ago when one of my friends described me as "the least able-to-be-controlled person that I know," and I started living right away.

Fast Bad Baby

When I was a baby I was fast and bad. I was born and my mother says I started walking around right away and she had to put bells on my feet so that she would know where I was going. I was born and I started moving around the space because I wanted to whip around in this world. I never wanted to go to sleep and my mother says I didn't have "first words" but instead I just started talking one day and I've never been able to be very quiet since then. Even in my dreams I talk and make a commotion. In the past, I was a baby and I was running around and my mother didn't know what to do because her baby was so rowdy and speedy compared to other babies she knew. She couldn't lock me up or tell me to slow down because I didn't know why I should listen to her and I just wanted to go fast, so what happened was that she put the little bells on my shoes and that way I was free to roam and she could hear me as I ran ringing through the house. With a bad and fast baby like me, the really worrisome thing would be when the jingles stopped. One time, before she put the bells on to track me, I climbed a dresser, using the drawers like stairs. One time I took a door off its hinges. One time I picked up a wild baby rabbit before it had a chance to run. One time I ate a thermometer. If you let me onto your land, I might be very wild, and I will not be able to totally change myself, but you can always track me by the tinkle of my lively clamor.

My Mother

Last summer, toward the end of a long walk, my mother went to the side of the dirt road and showed me a plant. I am used to having a rhythm with her in which she shows me something interesting in nature or architecture, and it's like a test: *Do you know what it is?* And it is very pleasing when I tell her what it is, and then we both enjoy that we both know.

Sometimes I *don't* know, and she likes the situation of me being "stumped" and she likes that she does know and can tell me what she knows. This is also one of the first ways that I perceived power in another person: Information about art and nature feels like the best stuff to have, and if you have it, it is powerful and excellent to pass it on. That is an act of power, showing what you know, giving it to another person, realizing that as you spread it, you get to keep it but watch it grow, and by watching others have it, you learn new things about the original thing.

I told my mother that the flower she showed me was a honeysuckle. I knew from the little conical, trumpet-shaped blooms. She nodded and we both knew that we knew. She picked a flower off and smelled it. Then she gave it to me to smell, and I sniffed in its honey-floral petal cone. It smelled like a fancy candy, and even though I'd smelled honeysuckle before, its scent pleasure-stung me anew, and I laughed a bit and said, "Unbelievable." She knew I was talking about the gentle shock you can feel about how straightforward nature is in its generosity, its dizzyingly intricate offerings.

I looked at my mother and asked her, "Do you want to smell it again?" But she shook her head and so I held the very small flower in my two hands and the position of my hands was like when Christian children say their bedtime prayers and I thought to start to try to make a prayer for this flower cone, but I also thought, *This is what makes my mother my mother. She loves the flower and she wants me to know this flower, but she will only smell it once, and then give it to me for unlimited sniffing pleasure and she will be happy about it all.*

I knew this to be true, and that the power of the flower had not just been its astounding smell or that I thought to create a prayer for it and consequently felt myself glow a bit, but that because of what happened between me and my mother and the small flower that we named and passed between us, my thoughts about how I saw her became an instantaneous prayer of gratitude and awe for her style of motherhood and unique humanity. And inside of myself, I knelt down in honor of this style of care that is her brand of nurturing, care that urges creativity and thinking, that is selfless and classy. It says, "The more you give, the more you have, the more new things you are a part of, the more you are truly alive." I held the fragile flower and made my footsteps the same level of noise as hers so that I could be with her like we were one entity. We walked on toward our house.

Deerhoof/Dream Deer

I'm a young woman who grew up in a haunted house in Massachusetts. Because of the ghosts in my house, I became a wild and fearful person who wants to protect others from pains but also expects all pains to fly right at me.

I'm so afraid of the dark in our house in Massachusetts that I sleep with the light on all night. I hold my pee in and sleep with my head under the blankets and sheets. In the morning, I peek out and then emerge, covered in sweat, exhausted, terrified, and full of pee. When I come down to breakfast, my mother says, "Oh, Jen. You look horrible," which is my mother's main way of saying that she loves me and remembers that I was once a baby that she controlled and I was a bad baby but she still loves me. She thinks that I look horrible because I am upset, because I drink too much alcohol and smoke too much pot, because I've been fired from my job, or dumped by a boyfriend, or because I've had a giant success and am gorging on it. But all it really is is that I've been up all night because I am afraid of ghosts.

I'm not afraid of curses or injuries that ghosts might do to me. I'm not afraid of the things that movies say that ghosts do, like lock the doors and windows, or show you what you would look like old, or make the present sour and moldy right before your eyes.

I'm specifically afraid of one thing: That they will watch me, and that they won't stop doing that. I'm afraid that I'll wake up and feel a creeping feeling, that I will let my eyes adjust to a darkness that is holding in a bad laugh, and that then there will be an old woman watching me, and that she won't blink enough, that she is strict, and that when my inner feelings want her to stop looking, or just do something else, she will start laughing at me. Basically, I am a comedian and actress who is afraid of people staring right at me, and only me, and then laughing. I'm not saying this because I feel bad for myself, or because I think that there is something wrong with me. I don't think that. I love myself. I think that I am a very top-quality person.

When I imagine my ingredients, I imagine that my muscles are made of plums, that my heart is a giant ruby with a light bulb in it, that my blood is goldenrod yellow, and the bones inside my body are made from lions' bones and shells, and that my brain is made of steak and silk and Hawaiian Punch. I don't have a problem with myself, really, I'm just afraid of ghosts, and because of my fear of ghosts, I sometimes have a problem when visiting my old home in Massachusetts.

The house in Massachusetts is big, surrounded by big lawns, which are surrounded by big woods. The house is a yellow colonial with smart green shutters, it has a large front porch, it has no air conditioning, and inside, my parents are in there, living with ghosts.

When you call my parents on the phone, this is what my father will say: "The tulips are really coming up. We had the rabbits eat a bunch of the bulbs, but we still managed to get so many flowers." And this is what my mother will say: "It's so sad. The rabbit must have been eaten by the fox, because there are so many more tulips than usual. The rabbit must have been eaten. There are too many tulips."

My mother thinks that there is just one of every animal in our woods. She is living in a fable world, where there are lessons and every animal means something. The Fox is a sneaky, skinny murderer who probably smokes cigarettes, can't grow a full beard like God can, and thinks pens with naked bikini ladies on them are funny. The lawn is a dangerous place for all of the animals because humans are natural predators, like in *Peter Rabbit*. The Deer is a promising young woman who works in an office and the Hawk is a kidnapper who can't control himself.

Now that my sisters and I are out of the house, there are even more animals around. When I was a teenager, I planted a vine of Concord grapes on the chain-link fence around the tennis court. I made a sign that said "Jenny's Grapes" and then never did anything else to it. The grapes worked, and in the fall there were a lot of them. They were all over the clay tennis court. "The Deer loves the grapes. She loves them and she eats them for lunch" is what my mother says, as if the Deer is a midtown office lady who comes in her ladies' suit, tennis sneakers, and tube socks and diet-lunches on the grapes.

One day in early November, the Deer comes to the court for her lunch break from her office job in the woods. She is a secretary for a tree. She clomps softly onto the court, the teal Har-Tru kicking up, and starts eating the now rotten grapes with her face. She wants more grapes, and so she steps closer to the fence. As she gets a new grape between her teeth, her Deerhoof gets stuck in the fence. It's gone through to the other side and she can't get it out. She struggles and struggles to get her foot out. She never goes back to the woods, because she struggles all afternoon and rests, then struggles throughout the night, and rests, and over the next few days, she gets weaker and weaker and more scared, and eventually she dies of a Deerheart attack, or of fright, or of just death from being so big and lying down too much.

Because it is November, nobody goes up to the tennis court, and also nobody goes up there because the court was built "for the girls," and now "the girls" have done the outrageous and unthinkable: They've become gigantic and can't fit into their baby clothes, they've wanted to go have sex, and so they've left. We really built the court for the girls. Our bodies hurt too much to go up there and have fun. So nobody goes up there.

A week or more after the Deer's deathly lunch break, my mother goes up there, maybe with the dog, who is now dead.

Here is the dog's life in a very short description: I went to the orthodontist, the orthodontist said I didn't have any canine teeth, my mother said to x-ray more of my head. They found the teeth up there in my head. I had braces for seven years, along with a terrible speech impediment and ugly face, accompanied by horniness that had started way before that and also never went away. At this time, we were allowed to get a hypoallergenic dog. We weren't allowed to take the dog upstairs. The dog was undisciplined because we only wanted to teach him how to hug, and he and my father were at war for thirteen years until the dog couldn't see or walk, and my father took good care of him and they became unlikely companions with a true bond. The dog's butthole fell out while he was pooping and they got an operation to put it back in. The butthole fell out again and because the dog was blind and his butthole was ruined and he was suffering from tumors and old age, they let the dog pass on.

But back in the time when he is still alive, my mother probably walks him up there and finds a giant dead Deer on the tennis court. Its eyes are open and it's just a huge mess. She has to call the animal control lady to come, the same lady who came for the rabid raccoons lolling on the lawn, and the coyote who pranked us by streaking through the yard. When the lady gets there, it's either this or that: This is that we cut a hole in the chain-link fence. That is that we cut the foot off of the dead Deer, saving the fence. Well, the Deer was already a goner, says my mother. "SO YOU CUT OFF THE FOOT?!" I scream. "Jen, we had to."

And in the aftertaste of what my mother says, I know she means, "Well, you were the person who planted the tempting grapes and then moved to New York and didn't get a home phone and makes us call you on your cell phone, which is only supposed to be for emergencies. You did that."

There is a feeling that by doing the natural thing of growing up, I have carelessly waltzed away from a mess. It feels that I have disowned my tribe by choosing to believe that the world is full of creatures and spirits rather than predators and ghosts.

When I go home, I sit and talk with my parents for hours. I love my parents. But now, especially now, when I go there, I hold in my pee and let out my sweat and squeeze my eyes tight because I am afraid of a ghost that is mine. It reflects my will to be wild, my inclination to plant roots, my hunger for treats, my fear that straying too far from the pack is what I must do but perhaps at a large cost.

When I wake up in the night, I know what I am scared to see: It is a three-footed deer, staring at me. Its eyes are eyes and then its eyes are grapes.

Restaurant

Hello, I am a woman on a blue and green sphere that has dollops and doinks of mountains all over it. Some of the mountains on my cosmic sphere splooge out thick liquid fire spurts that run downhill and cool and turn into vacation destinations after a few thousand years. I am a woman living on a planet that has noodle-shaped guys squiggling silently in the soil and four-legged mammal-kings with hammer feet, or horns on their heads, or coats covered in spots and stripes, and my planet has live feathered beaky skeletons flying through the environment, and big heavy creatures who are tusked and trunked and have sad long memories and wash their bodies with cold mud puddles and know who their babies are.

There are large deadly cats watching everything in the dark, sneaking through the fanned-out ferns. There are delighted pigs and gossiping geese and dogs that sit with their mouths open so that they can cool off after running around. There are arrows of extra electricity ripping through the air, loud drum noises in the sky when two opposite temperatures collide, deep wide dents filled with water and populated by animals that have scales or blowholes or no eyes or live in shells that look like tiny hard purses made out of little plates. There are white puffs floating in the air here; they float high above my house. The puffs turn into wet water-bloops and fall down and turn my hair from straight to curly. The water-bloops also make the flowers open up, they turn dust to mudslides, they intercept a sunbeam and make an arch that you can't touch because it is made of swoops of colored light.

Hello? Tonight I am going to the Restaurant, where I will eat a killed and burned-up bird and drink old purple grapes and also I will gulp clear water that used to have bugs and poop and poison in it but has been cleaned up so that it doesn't make us blow chunks. Oh Joy I am going to the Restaurant and I am just drooling at the thought of the killed and burned bird and I want to sip the grape gunk and so I put skin-colored paint all over my face and I dab pasty red pigment on my lips and swish peachy powder on my cheeks and I take a pencil and draw an eye-shaped line around my eye so that people know where my blinkers are.

And then I take a little brush and I slick black paint over each eyelash and then I take a hot metal stick and wind my head-hairs around it so that everything is spirals. I stuff each breast into a cotton cup-bag, and the bags are sewn together as a pair of bags for boobs, and the pair of boob-bags is held on by straps because I guess this helps the boobs from not floating past the mountains and white puffs and into outer space?

This is the right way to appear if you want to go out of the house and go to the Restaurant and not have to stay home and be alone forever, which, on Earth, is bad.

Inside the cotton-cups my nipples press like bright coins against the boundaries of the bags because they want to be out and on a beach and not in bags, and they would gladly pay to be set free, but I can't give any money toward freedom because my money is for the Restaurant tonight.

I cover my body with a fabric that has been made into a certain shape to help remind you of my butt and vagina, but it does not show the actual butt or vagina that I have. Hello, I am a woman here on this ancient ball that rotates with a collection of other balls around a bigger ball made up of lights and gasses that are science gasses, not farts. Don't be immature. I wear this paint and these bags and this butt-vagina fabric-map so that I can be here on the globe and go to places like the Restaurant. At the Restaurant I pay with my money that I earn from pretending to be *other women.* I get that money so that I can afford all of the face paint and boob-bags that I need to put on so that I can go to the Restaurant and eat the dead burned bird and gargle the purple grape gloop that sometimes makes me fall down or throw up all over this globe. This is the cycle that I rotate through so that I can go to more places on this sphere as it rotates through eternal darkness and endless space.

Daydreams/Tides

A day at the beach was never so dull as it is now.

I recycle the same daydreams over and over—

This man decides that indeed I am the one to love and so he travels to where I live. He travels far, directly to my front door, thinking of me the whole time that he is moving across the country and across the sky. He thinks of me as he puts on his clothes, as he buys coffee in the airport, thinking, "It doesn't feel normal to buy coffee before something so huge! It feels like I should be buying a cloud or a star. I can't believe I'm in normal life but also, I hope, about to begin this huge love. Maybe one day I will tell her about this experience."

He has packed his toothbrush. It feels like pleasure to him but also too urgent, it feels like starving as he thinks about how full he would feel, how filling it would be to stand next to me in his pajamas and me in my pajamas and us both using our toothbrushes, looking at ourselves and each other in the mirror.

He thinks that it is so precious that he knows that it would be a privilege to be allowed in to my evening. He thinks in layers when he thinks about how he loves me.

He travels all the way to my edge of the country. He touches down, speeds forward until he stands at the gate to my house and he sees me doing something dear and useful but also related to my belief in adornment, like watering my geraniums or talking to the dog and saying something to the dog like, "Aren't you happy about the softness in the air today? That's what they call balmy." And he sees as I bend closer to the dog and he sees down my shirt and I touch the dog's velveteen ear and I say very softly and in a very rich tone, "Balmy."

Or he sees me pay no mind to anyone but myself as I carry my groceries. He sees me being satisfied and self-sufficient. He sees me as myself when nobody is watching, except that he is watching.

I repeat and repeat the daydream. But now the fantasy person makes no sense, because he is an amalgamation of my different recent loves, who have all been terribly disappointing and irredeemable, which is a big blow to my romantic inclinations, because I do love a comeback.

But they are not allowed to come back because they have been very bad.

Now the man is simply too disappointing to even be in a daydream, because daydreams are many things but most substantially they are flares of faith and for me they are wishes that happen through feelings rather than saying "I wish so and so would be here and love me."

Now, the man can't even be wished for. The facts are too firm. The man would have to be someone other than who he is and he is simply and only himself, no matter which one of the men he is.

I have encountered nothing but a flock of flimsy fools, I say, with a bad attitude.

So now there is not even anyone to dream about, and what an odd feeling. I don't have the strength to put together the features of a fantasy face. I am heartbroken over no one, over having nobody to wish for, nobody to hope for. I am heartbroken, usually, over someone. Now I am heartbroken over no one.

I have nobody to serve. I have nobody to please me or

to please. I can't even dream my daydreams, to give to myself, because I have always done them this way, with the materials for the daydream being a certain man. Life has been so discouraging that I have forgotten why and how to fantasize, and I feel weak.

The structure of what I wish for and the images that usually come together for me to be happy have to change now. But what am I supposed to do with all of the parts of my heart that are only there to be given? What am I supposed to do with all of this nothing that I see? Those parts of the heart, they really aren't for me, they are not for my home or my body or my self-love. They are for you, and wherever you are, you are too unknown to be in my daydream. You are on the fringe of my wish for someone to wish for. You are in another country of the heart. You are on the very outskirts of the edge of where my waves hit. You are on a beach on the other side of another world.

All I can do is believe in the tides, the big drawing in and drawing out that is a type of planet clock. All I can do is let the waves of this whole damn thing flood in and out. If I could remember anything, I would remember my belief that my extra love could just be used on myself. But when I stop feeling pleasure and stop imagining things I also forget my beliefs, the things that float my spirit on this sea.

When my beliefs float my spirit on the sea, I imagine the depths beneath me and all of the options for life in there. I can feel, with relief, the wideness of the sea. I can remember that things from faraway locations wash up right on your private wedge of sand and present themselves as yours right away. But I have had my heart broken once again, and I am exhausted, and I have forgotten that I can still give to myself. And so I sit here with waves crashing and repeating, and all I can do is wait and hope that eventually my sea will cough up some shell with a shape like a swirl of sound and I will look anew and I will listen better.

But this afternoon it is this: A day at the beach was never so dull as it is now. Without a person to love, I am too full of what must be let out, and while at least I can use my mind enough to bring out this image of this sea, it feels like life is the beach in the winter. It feels like life is the beach where I used to go with someone who died. It feels almost wrong to be here . . . I feel like I am wearing a bikini and the weather is forty degrees and the sky is that screaming winter white and it is all I can do to just stand still and try to remember why I am here. It is all I can do to not pack up and leave.

I Want to Look Out a Window

I want to look out a window at something bright and wide, and at that point accept my nature and understand my intended use and have a clean shirt and clean hands and feel similar to a small planet.

I want to be in a fine wooden house by the sea and to have a big sweater.

I want to be a baby fawn on the lawn, to have spots on my coat that remind people of a mousse-y and chilled refrigerator dessert, and also shock onlookers by reminding them of how young things are able to be, so young that they are closer to energy than flesh.

When people get a glimpse of me I'd like them to feel like it is a good omen.

I want to have a face with dirt on it. I want to jump on people!

I'm beginning to suspect that I swallowed a roller-coaster and it is lodged between my heart and my stuff.

Am I too big or too small or too much or too little?

I have always known that I would die for love. I think I am dying while or because of waiting for it. I cannot bear how it feels like a surging throng of beats and yells and gasps inside of my small form. I have wondered on many occasions if any confidence I have is just a weird side effect of foolishness and I live under the weight of so much embarrassment, I'm surprised the top of my head isn't flat.

If I planted my pussy in the ground right now it would grow into a tree of flaming swords with a moat of tears around it.

What is my diagnosis?

I Died: Valentine's Day

Well, I just died.

What do they say? They say, "That's that."

Yes. That is that.

I woke up and it was Valentine's Day and I was lying in my bed and my body was the shape of a melting chair. I was actually just a melting chair with nobody left to sit in it. I was a useless ruined form yelling *SIT ON ME PLEASE PUT YOUR WEIGHT ON ME* in a worthless pointless voice that sounded like a fart under the covers.

Sometimes there is something mean living in me and

this mean thing gets a sick pleasure from harsh punish-
ment and frightening imagery about who I am or what I
should do.

I experience a lot of difficulties.

I died that day that I knew was Valentine's Day and I
knew it was Valentine's Day because it has always been
my goal to be in love and to get a proper valentine and
to not be lonely but to have someone who loves me so
much that they miss me when I'm not there.

A psychic recently looked right into the eternal cosmos and then returned to me with this elegant yet cryptic
message: Grow up.

I'm stuck here in a cycle and I am getting older but
I am not growing up and my heart is getting soft dark
spots on it like a fruit that has gone bad or is soft because
too many hands have squeezed it but then put it back
down not because I am not ready but because they were
not ready for my type of fruity flesh. I felt so ripe and
sweet—what was off? The truth is, I was forcing myself
into people's mouths. I jumped out of their hands and
into their mouths and I yelled *EAT ME* way before they
even had a chance to get hungry and notice me and lift
me up.

I died and it was Valentine's Day and I was saying "I
ruined everything," because that's what the meanie in me

wanted me to say and I had no more strength to stop that sappy speech.

I was using all of my strength to be a melting chair.

I stayed there in the shape of the bad chair and I thought about how I used to have a husband and we had a few absolutely A+ Valentine's Days. But that was not enough. *Grow. Up.*

I stayed in the shape of the melting chair and I didn't protect myself at all. I wasn't careful while the cruel part of my psyche dealt me these thoughts. I let it get so far that soon the thoughts were not just within me but were the main citizens of my world and they were mobilizing and marching to get me.

They came up from under the bed, they wrapped my body up, they pushed my eyes in and choked me. I had only a few breaths left and it was enough of a clear emergency, the kind of emergency that can cause an end. I made myself get out of my dead bed and I said, *You stop being this chair now!*

But it was too late and when I went to the bathroom to look in the mirror to see if I was very sick or not, I saw dark circles not just around my eyes but all around my life and I did think things like *If you die, nobody will care for the dog,* and other things like *You're not even good at caring for the dog and he's bored with you and your beauty is gone and you didn't appreciate it when you had it and you're still too dumb to even locate when that window of beauty even was.*

Soon my face was just two dark brown circular indents with a fish mouth.

I thought about how one Valentine's Day an old bad boyfriend gave me his own old digital camera and stuck it in a sock so that I *could unwrap it,* and then he went out and bought himself a new camera, and then we broke up a few months later. And you know what? I have been waiting for a good love for a really long time and I have been lying in order to be a part of something for almost forever, and actually it feels better to just give the whole thing a big *NO THANK YOU* in the form of passing right away.

I stood on a spot between the bathroom and bedroom and I said to the bossy eternal cosmos, *Well, just let me go. Just let me go. I am tired of sinking down to a lower place to be with men. I am tired of throwing a tarp over some of my personality so that the shape of my identity suits some gross man a little better, for whatever shitty things he needs to do in order to keep his boring identity erect and supreme. I have many grievances and no place to set them down, and I am cranky from having to shoulder this burden of reactions, like I am a fucking Ox that should carry your unsellable wares. I am tired of buying my own flowers. I am tired of having to hold my breath through Valentine's Day the way you do when you drive past a graveyard. I want a valentine from a normal person who is horny. I want a prize for how well I can love. I want to be a prize for love.*

And you know what? I thought it all and it was sour but full of energy and I looked at the dog and said, *Will you be my valentine?* And just like every other man I'd met so far he couldn't exactly understand me but he winced at my tone and just like every other man he was ruining my house and so I let the brown circles overtake me because at least when you die it is not your job to hold all of these dark disks for everyone anymore.

And I took pity on the little dog and gathered him to my chest with my rotten-grocery-store-plum heart and I used my last bit of whatever I had to just make myself die. I turned into the only circle of light and it didn't even feel great or like liberation and I just floated up and lightly bonked the ceiling and then I sank back down and settled on the floor and I just admitted that I love Valentine's Day and nobody loves me and I'm horny and nobody is here and I just died.

The small circle of myself lay there on the floor between the two rooms that are for shitting and sleeping.

But what is so hard is that even when I die my light still stays on.

44

Ghosts

When my parents moved in to our house in Massachusetts, the house I grew up in, it was filled with the furniture of the dead people who lived there before, and maybe with some of the stuff of the dead lady who lived there before the most recent dead couple. Layers of deaths. They had to clear a lot of things out and away. They had to make it their own. My mother was getting wheezy because of the dusty runner on the stairs, and so she and my father decided to rip it up. When they did this, they discovered a package, or maybe a few packages of letters. They were love letters. They were written to someone who had lived in the house, but they weren't from the person's spouse; they were from someone else. An other.

It's a little gossipy and scary to tell this story, because my parents knew the descendants of the dead, of the person who had had this extra love. Therefore, they also knew the descendants of the person who knew nothing about *their love's* extra love, but walked up and down on the words of that love every day, not knowing that little strips of their partner's heart were underneath their feet, promised to someone else.

The letters were written by a man who sailed the seas. He was a sea captain. A *male* male, maybe stoic and rough, so that he could stand the seas, but still crackable even while craggy, because he had been caught up in this forbidden love. My father took the letters to his office, thinking that he would write about them.

This is the first step toward seeing a ghost: Discovery followed by meddling. Taking something into your life, something that is clearly a powerful object from another's life experience. That night, or a few nights later, my mother smelled my father's pipe smoke. It was late at night and she called out for him to come to bed, but when she turned over, my father was there, snoozing away. So she said, "You left your pipe burning. You're going to burn down this new old house that we just bought." But my father said that he hadn't smoked his pipe that night. My mother then came to the natural conclusion that there was a robber in our house, and that the robber was smoking a pipe while he stole our things.

My father went out into the hallway, to do what to the robber? I'm not sure. But what happened was this: My father stood there in the hall, smelling that pipe smell, and watched as a sea captain–type person smoked a pipe and climbed the stairs. My father says that he saw the man, but didn't see him, but saw him. I don't know what my father said to my mother, but somehow she ended up knowing that he had seen a ghost, which is not great for anyone, especially a couple with a young daughter asleep in her bed.

My father knew somebody who knew some things about ghosts. This person said the thing that now we all know is true about ghosts: "They have unfinished business. Those letters aren't any of your business. Burn the letters and the ghost will go away." And he did. He, my father, burned the letters, and he, the ghost, went away, as far as I know. But sometimes we would smell the smell, and I would wonder why it was coming back at just that moment.

My mother and sister also saw the form of a woman wander out of the den and ascend toward the light fixture in the hall, but I can't seem to find any connection to that story except that it is terrifying, and I put it on my list of events that I'm glad I missed.

But back to the sea captain and his broken heart. I somehow always felt that this was my story as well. Maybe because I was so obsessed with what it would feel like to one day fall in love, to have another person who loved you the most, and loved you so much, voluntarily, that it became involuntary. I thought of what his ghost brain must be saying. Was he sad and mad, saying, "You made me live without you and so I died this way, living without you, looking for you. And now I am quite literally dead on my feet." I think I am afraid of this happening to me. Taking the risk, believing that love and its people are not predatory, and being a part of the sharing of hearts, only to have to be separated and spend all of my living life waiting for the sharing to really turn into the joining of hearts.

Each time I fall in love I feel fear that the world won't let me be in the world with it, that I either have to pick the world or the love. Did the sea captain pick the love, and now he regrets that choice? Is he stuck walking up a staircase for all eternity, stepping with each step on the words that he sent with all his heart, crushing them under his own invisible foot, feeling his real heart break? Did he choose love and it didn't take, and now is he stuck in the world without the love, forever?

I didn't fall in love until many years after I left the house. Sometimes I would fall in love and it would fall apart, and I would return to the house to catch my breath, still alive, still alive. I don't know what makes a ghost a ghost and why they seem to be interned in a weird, repetitive, emotionally fueled prison. I spent so much time in my childhood trying to figure out why the ghost was even in our house, considering that during his life he was probably on a big wooden boat most of the time. Maybe he came to our house one afternoon and they had an affair in our house, in one of the bedrooms where we all slept like normal people.

Maybe he never came to our house, but came there in death, because he followed his letters, essentially following his heart. Maybe he was trying to get his heart back from our house. I get that. I get why he would go back there for his heart. I love the house, and every time I go out into the world and get my heart busted up, I retreat back to the old ghostly house in Milton, hoping to become myself again, and to have one more chance, just one more chance to share my heart, and to share it successfully enough that if I become a ghost one day, there's at least another ghost right beside me. And I have its heart and it has mine, and we had the world together. This is what I believe can happen to me. I don't know if I believe in ghosts, but I believe that this can happen to me.

Color-Spirit

I am told that I should try to date online. My reaction to this is that I want to walk away so forcefully that I don't even pause to open the door, I just go through the wall. I will never ever go into the internet to look for anything that I feel that I really need, except for turtlenecks and sheets and candles, and even then I will do that in a very small circle of places that I know have exactly what I want. But I want to fall in love, so I'll give it an earnest try. Here are a few bios:

Version 1: Jenny Slate
Human Woman, Los Angeles, USA, Earth
About Me:

Hi!

I know where the confusion starts, because I am a woman and I do look like one but the real truth is that I am a *Color-Spirit*. And it says on many documents that I come from here but actually I am a citizen of *The World of Shapes*. That is where I'm from and *The World of Shapes* is the place where they speak my mother tongue.

All day I do my loving, and all of my feelings are colors and they are shapes and they are shapes of colors, when you get really deep into my experience. I am a creature who is classified in the universal records as a *Color-Spirit*. I watch the light make tones.

I feel a thing and tell myself what shape it is.

My physical heart feels so exposed, so shallowly planted. It feels like it is in my mouth. I can't tell if I'm spitting it out or swallowing it. I can't tell if I'm going to chomp it to bits just by trying to be here. My physical heart seems to be blasting light out of my mouth but also down into my body. I fear that when the light is shining directly out of my face that nobody will want to or even be able to look at me.

I have many beats at once. I have the beats of that bloody, smooth physical heart. I also rock with the beats of colors and shapes. I rumble with the beats of the private language of those two separate hearts, the language that they have created between them. You could understand, then, why it's so hard for me to keep still, how even when I am still, I am bopping microscopically.

There cannot, there certainly may not, be one more man, not even one more man for a night, not one more who comes in and doesn't feel in himself what I am about, there cannot be one more person who absentmindedly swats at my little triangles and squares as they swim and bob in the air. There may not be one more man who turns his own face away in fear and ignorance from the colors that make him angry because I can see them and he cannot.

I am the real *Color-Spirit*.

I love spicy food and pints of beer. I like the beach. I like dogs. I don't like rock climbing or other sports that seem like you do them in Colorado. I hate it when people judge other people about being athletic. Computers are not good. I like to get joyfully shitfaced with close friends at least once every month. I don't care much for air-conditioning. A bathrobe is a wonderful present, so is jam, so are flowers.

Who will meet me at once in all of my worlds and pump with all of my hearts? To have to kill even one of my hearts to match up with you is simply not worth it to me, after all that has happened. Hit me up if you feel me!

Version 2: Jenny?
Mammal, Awake, America, Universe
About Me:

Whoops!

I am a plant and I have a fragile green stem and my flower is still in the pod on the top of the stalk, unopened, when the dawn strolls in over the horizon. My blossom spreads out during the day and it goes into the pod at night and then it goes again the next day and all of the days.

I am a young woman and I am also a spirit of many translucent tones and classic forms of ferns. I am so delicate, so delicate that I am the one the ghosts know not to spook. I don't need the shock of the apparition of an actual ghost in order to believe in the other worlds. I am in all of them and I know where my deepest home is. It is a dimension populated by plants and all of the colors that you can know, and the gods are called Ferns of Faith and I am very religious about them. I'm from there. How afraid are you of this? Or do you want more?

I have my whole stem and this is what I am and what it is. I am the tender stem. Who is the sun who will return every day just to make sure I open up, and who will give me my own dark evening to close and just be within?

I like the sound of bugs talking to each other outside in the night.

I think the air smells best when all of the tree smells get swirled up by a storm. Big old trees on my street listen to me and watch me in a nice way like I am their niece.

The plants and flowers in my window boxes just space out and sigh. I'd estimate that I have spent about forty-five percent of my lifetime spacing out. What do you do?

Okay. End?

Version 3: Me
Morning, House, Now
About Me:

I am supposed to be touched. I can't wait to find the person who will come into the kitchen just to smell my neck and get behind me and hug me and breathe me in and make me turn around and make me kiss his face and put my hands in his hair even with my soapy dishwater drips. I am a lovely woman. Who will come into my kitchen and be hungry for me?

I make it very obvious what the right way to treat me is. If you don't think it's important to hold hands and you are lukewarm about snuggling, don't bother sniffing around my stall.

It would be great if you are not weird in one way or another about what your mother did or how you feel about your penis but I know that is a lot to ask.

Personality types not preferred: Know-it-alls, meanies, grumps, vultures, spoileds, piggies, and especially bullies.

Preferred: Lovebugs, creatures, boo-boos, rigorous thinkers, wild-hearts, gentle-minds, pets.

This exercise is actually too sad to do.

All I want to do is disappear deeply into my own thing and you can decide whether or not to join but I'm pretty much going to enter my own vortex.

But are you there? Please come close enough so

that I can see you, and then I will try to do the rest for both of us, because I have not learned my lesson yet and do not possess the faith to believe in the partner who does his side of the thing. But I would love it if you would, because that would be dreamy and then I would also have that faith.

I will give you every single treat.

Letter: Dreams

Dear Ms. Slate,

It has come to our attention that you recently created a dream in which you were waiting in line for a sandwich, and that this was the whole dream.

As if that is not enough, there is a concerning report that your subconscious also produced a *tensionless seven-hour dream* about *watching an airplane land during the day* and that, again, this was all that happened. There was not even a sunset or a sense of where the plane was landing, and apparently the message of the dream was, *Nothing cared that nothing cared.*

Really, Ms. Slate, this is starting to feel difficult.

To be clear, nobody is asking for you to go back to *Dracula disguises himself as a Frog and waits at the end of the bed for you and only you, and obviously you go right up to "Frog-Dracula" because "frogs indoors who don't run away and frogs who only want to be friends and sit at the edge of the bed are a real stroke of luck," but then right when you get to the Frog he turns back into Dracula and you are fooled into being killed by him, and he is laughing at you because he tricked you, and just before you die, you realize that you hate the idea of being tricked more than you actually hate the idea of dying, and you also realize that you are afraid of "getting yourself sucked out of yourself" by a man who is dressed in a tuxedo, which is usually an outfit for a classy man at a fancy party, but really Dracula is just vain and thirsty and there is no party and he is nothing but a bitchy, life-drinking, life-draining liar.*

There is no conversation internally to suggest that we go that route again.

Nor are we inclined to revisit *You are an archeologist and you are wearing all khaki including a khaki explorer-hat thing and bad long shorts with crotch puff, and you are at a flea market/book fair that has been set up in a school gym in England in 1970, and you stumble upon an artifact from the "way before past," and this artifact is a pencil sketch of a staring woman, and then you look closely and realize that it is you, like, it's your soul, and the message is vague but far from positive about your lifetime(s), and there is a sourness or curse regarding romantic stuff and the curse is attached to your interlife spirit, and the picture sends something that feels like "the energy of bile but not actual barf" from the picture up to your terror-frozen face and gaping mouth, and you wake up so rigid with fear that your body feels like a bunch of found objects that are the following: parts of a broken rocking chair, old spoons, and chains from the swings on swing sets.*

I think we can all agree that if that's our only other option, then we should just shut this whole thing down.

And to be totally frank, we can't even find the language to approach *You go into the first-class section of an airplane and a man who represents an amalgamation of all your exes is somewhere on the plane, and you do not have a ticket for first class, and you find that the seats in first class are not seats but normal-sized brown plastic beds with white sheets, and you do not have a ticket but you still get in one of the beds and pull the covers up and hold the top of the covers between your teeth and you feel the linen in your mouth, drying up the parts of the mouth that it touches so that it would be too painful to speak, and then you casually and completely go to the bathroom in the bed, you poop in the bed with a neutral attitude while lying flat on your back with a dry, linen-stuffed mouth.* We can't, as they say, dignify that dream with a response.

While we're not quite at that point of ending your dream-life experience, we do need to have an honest discussion about this upsetting situation. The laziness and deeply boring nature of the *waiting in line for sandwich* dream is simply not something that we can tolerate, and it would do us all a disservice to sweep it under the rug. The *airplane landing in day* dream is discouraging, especially after all we've been through. The *airplane first-class movement* dream—as it has been labelled internally—has understandably caused great alarm and sadness.

Please come in and see us at your earliest convenience so that we can dialogue about this.

Sincerely,
The Committee for Evening Experiences

PS: Speaking of "sweeping things under the rug,"
I don't think you'd hear even a peep of objection
if we were to have a repeat of *Rug turns into carpet
of flowers that are alive and you can wear the whole
thing as a shawl and new blooms keep popping even
as you walk casually through a cocktail party at the
house of a nice older woman who supports your
work.* There have also been numerous requests for
*You are in the passenger seat of a van, sitting on the
lap of a real dog who is the size of and style of Barkley
from* Sesame Street, *and he is sitting like a person
and you are on his lap and he is hugging you because
he loves you and you are sharing a seatbelt and it is
the time of year that is the seasonal bridge between
spring and summer.*

Trench-Times/Dream Dog

I know that thing, that thing of waking up but it's all tinted gray and your blood is paste and your heart is a boring rock. I know that thing that has no voice but sucks the sound out, wasting it, not using it, leaving you either pale or red-faced. I know the gray thing.

There were the big problems: One man was gone from my life just about the time that another man pig-snorted his way into the presidency. And that made all of the littler problems much harder to face. I was downtrodden and, to my surprise, felt that having a good attitude was no longer worth it. I could not identify what was worthy and what was not. I didn't know how or why to give myself small pleasures. Something would happen like I wouldn't get a part in a film or I would cancel a show due to stage fright and I would just stay down at the bottom of the experience. I used to float up. Now I was just flipping out, flopping down.

For a while I would have trench-times when everything felt like blank paper and I couldn't feel anyone's heart pointed even in my direction, let alone anyone loving me or wanting me to be around. Very boring, very lonely, very tired, *again*. It was hard to feel anything, except *I am not one of the creatures who will experience anything precious*. Trench-times were shallow, heavy, and mean. I couldn't get into the actual morning because I was stuck underneath the weight of my days.

One night I had a dream that I was sitting on the lap of a giant dog. We were in the front seat of a van and the window was open and the weather was fair. The dog was hugging me with great squeezes and we were sharing a seatbelt.

When I woke up I was inclined to throw away my joy because *it is not real* but then something in me jumped from deep below where I must have cast it down. I was always yelling *Get down!* to my resilience when I was in my trench-times. But the thing did not get down—in fact, it came up and out, blazing. This thing inside of me, encouraged by the dream of the nice good dog, yelled out, *Your feelings of joy are not fake if you are having them! You are allowed to feel joy about sitting on the lap of a dog in a dream, and taking a ride in a van with open windows and sharing a seatbelt. God dammit, this is a gift from your fucking soul! Self-generate, don't you see? Break the trap break the trap break the trap leave the trench! Activate the bomb in yourself and bust out, trick yourself out of that trench in any way you can!*

I eventually got out of the bed, and there I was. I was out of the bed. I just got right out of the bed even though there was nothing to do and I was still very tired. My chest was laced through with an ever-tightening web of anxiety that was also reaching up into my throat and pressing my mouth down into a frown shape. I felt that nobody should see this posture of emotional twisting, this sour-seeming palsy, including myself. I could not even look at myself.

The only thing left was the number zero.

I spoke to myself in the voice of the giant dog from the dream.

Open a window up for yourself.

I found a window that opened.

There you are, do you know what you are doing? You are finding the new air for yourself. What a useful, good action to take. You are a person who got up and found the air. Take at least ten breaths. It's a fact that this is the main thing that you need to do to stay alive, breathing, and now it is a treat. Look at you! You have done what the earliest geniuses have done: You have taken the most basic thing and elevated it. If you are sweet inside of yourself for the most part, this is the truth you will know.

I started to spend my extra time caring for myself in little ways that reminded me of the generosity of my dream-dog who shared his seatbelt. The big pet. My dream-dog. I think he was training me in my dreams so that I could eventually play well in my days.

Eclipse

I went outside of my hotel to watch the highly anticipated eclipse of the sun. It happened. The sun was
eclipsed. All of the people were out on the sidewalk in
New York City, sharing little eyeglasses made of paper,
with the plastic lenses. I had no paper glasses. I saw a
stranger and I looked shyly at the glasses he had and I
asked, "Can I try?" The stranger gave me his glasses so
that I could watch the sun become a strange orange fang
poking through one side of the sky. A stranger helped
me. Specifically, he helped me look into outer space. I

said thank you, obviously. Related question: After this eclipse and group experience, is everyone else's hair also made out of necklaces now and is your heart a plum with a golden marble in it that will spin eternally, like mine is? Final comment: It is very warming to think of the adults going to places to get the paper glasses, and to think of the adults who own a small store or bodega, and that they heard about the eclipse and then ordered the paper glasses, knowing that people would want to watch the rare thing that was going to happen.

Touch vs. Smack

I don't want to smack anything on the ass and say
LET'S GO.

I want to touch something on the side of the face and say
WILL YOU PLEASE TAKE ME?

I Died: Listening

I died.

Oh, god! I did die!

Some man was standing right in the middle of the room talking about how he knew that *now was the time for men to listen,* and he was proud to say that he knew how to listen but strangely he kept talking for so long and *I* was the one who was listening and so then what happened was that my head twisted around on my neck and faced the wall.

But that didn't seem to bother him and it certainly

didn't stop him because I guess he was on a roll? And then he just walked around to the other side of me and kept talking, and what he was saying was so obvious but backward and wrong, but to tell him that would have caused a big bust-up.

And even though my head was on backwards and my brain felt, you know, not at its best, I was still aware that two very bad choices were being shoved at me: Tell him that he's right or at least on the right track and therefore lie and also abandon myself and cause more damage by letting his ignorance and monologue go on forever, or tell him NO, he is not even close to correct, that the fact that he is pontificating and instructing and not actually conversing is a sign that he does not even remotely understand. But then after saying *that* I would have to weather the storm of his humiliation and frustration, and somehow end up feeling bad about myself, like I should have been gentler and treated him like a child who simply doesn't know any better.

Or should I have been grateful that he was interested in *talking about listening* at all? But then again, he was demanding to be treated like a *man* who *does* know how to listen, while he was asking me to only listen to him and lie to him and maybe give him a prize? And I was so chilled by the reality of having to choose between bad and worse that my heart became flash-frozen and then it cracked in half and so what I'm saying is that basically my heart broke almost right away.

I thought, "Oh, great. Now I've got a backwards head and a broken thingy."

I tried to sit very still but inside of me the blood couldn't go around because there was no working heart to pump it, and he was still talking, even still, and what happened then was that my backwards head, which was already under a fair amount of stress from facing the wrong side of my body and only offered a bad view, which was the man, mostly the man, and then the wall—well, my backwards head sort of tore off at the neck and dangled down, just hung there for quite a while, which was unsightly and embarrassing.

Oh no! I didn't want to look ugly!

The man was getting irritated because I guess I was *making a face* and *rolling my eyes,* but what was hard about that was that my head was dangling upside down and so my eyeballs *were,* to be fair, rolling around. He started to ask tense, defensive questions to which the an- swer was clearly supposed to be "No, no, the problem is not *you, it's other worse men who do crimes and things like that,"* even though it *was* him and it is probably all of us. All.

As my eyes rolled back in my head and I saw into my own mind, I caught a glimpse of some old messages scrawled on the walls in there, and I thought, "The bad thing has gotten into all of us and we all need to get it out of us." And when I started to think about how it is certainly all of us that have a bit of this bad thing in us, the shards of my frozen heart really began to prick at me, and my dangling head became as heavy as a wrecking ball.

And then my head just completely disengaged from the rest of me. It fell off and it bonked down onto the floor. I felt it roll slightly away but I didn't know how far it had gone and that was stressful because I wanted to have some control over my head.

I didn't want to be rude by kneeling down and feeling around on the floor for the head, because that might make it seem like I was distracted or not listening, and the man was already so strangely angry even though I was the one falling to pieces and everything he was saying was in favor of keeping himself *together* and also never changing.

Even though everything he was saying was being said to dismantle and delegitimize the humane system I believed in, the one that demands equal rights and good old-fashioned empathy, the one that would strip him of his excessive privileges, the one that celebrates things being various, multi, plural, open, and requires him to explore being truly vulnerable. I wanted him to understand that "being vulnerable" is a different thing for everyone, is a developed and specific skill involving personally specific actions that are terrifying.

But I couldn't really get a word in edgewise, as they say.

I really did feel concerned about where my head might be and I could feel my blood as it stalled inside of myself. I was taking a breath maybe every three minutes and I started to worry that, you know, this was not going to work out for me, because that's just not enough. It's nowhere near the amount of breaths that he was getting to suck in and snort out.

But then again, I didn't want to seem like I wasn't being attentive, because recently I had let the man in on the terrible secret, which is that many men interrupt and disregard women and do it religiously and don't even notice that they're doing it but also gain power by doing it even if they do it without thinking, without what I guess you would call "consideration." And so now if I ever interrupted the man, he would tell me in my own language how painful it is to be interrupted. He would explain, in a voice that sounded so much like my own, how I am not considerate, even though I am considering a lot.

And yes, that would confuse me, because he would sound just like me, even though he wasn't me and had never had any of my experiences or experiences even much like my own. I was now in a position of being a hypocrite if I didn't "honor his experience of my experience." In an effort to be helpful, I had revealed the terrible secret, and I guess it made the man feel so scared and defensive that all he could do was to appropriate my whole experience as his and then accuse me of starting the problem.

My eyes were still rolled back in my head, which was somewhere on the floor, so I couldn't see it but I heard him say that he felt "unseen." It is hard to even describe what it's like to have someone use your own revelation of suffering as a way to accuse you of being cruel.

And it doesn't even matter because my head fell off and I'm dead now, but I must say: I really did not start it. No woman started it, by the way. I can say, safely, from the comfort of the great beyond, that Patriarchy and Misogyny are neither the fault nor the invention of women. Get out of here. Get out. Get right out of my life with that and get the hell out of my death with it. Let me rest in peace and quiet.

Where was I? Oh yes yes yes, so then, even though my head was lost on the floor somewhere and the thoughts had spilled out, some of them were trying to jump back up to me. But in general it was a poor showing and the thoughts I got ahold of didn't seem to really go with each other and I gave up. But just when I was about to surrender to the whole experience and accept that my head had gotten away from me for good, I realized what was happening. I took it seriously, and from my head on the floor I screamed, "I see that you are trying to kill me! I see it!"

And then I saw the whole of the thing that had happened, not just to me but to so many people, and I... Well, honestly, it was so incredibly overwhelming that I just stopped caring about what he thought and I went right ahead and felt around and finally found my head and I cradled my own head in my arms. My face nuzzled into my breasts and my hands stroked my own brow and I comforted myself, in pieces. I looked up past my heart and past my former headspace and into the sky, and my mouth still had a voice and it murmured to my heart, "It doesn't have to be like this."

And then I died.

And actually I have no idea what he did. He might still be talking, so if you are alive out there, I'd advise you to try to keep your head.

Beach Animals

We were on an Island. The two women arrived by plane, dressed in matching joke outfits that they'd bought in the city where I used to live, where I was born. I thought about how they'd had a discussion somewhere on the other side of the bay and decided to buy these raspberry-colored outfits with their own money. They'd taken off their normal clothes and changed into these new things, not just to please me, but to jostle me with this ridiculous surprise. I saw them and I saw their faces watching my face to see if I liked what they did. I experienced a celebration inside of myself, like I remembered what it was like to win something.

The women were new friends but I loved them in a massive way. The love was like a large trove of devotion that could only be amassed over time, but it had arrived all at once. The way I loved them felt like it was from long ago. Seeing them always felt like a reunion even though we didn't have a *before* before this. Hearing them say anything, hearing either one of them reveal something specific about herself made me feel downright ecstatic. It is not wrong to say that something was happening. I drove them in the car and we were all exploding.

We all went into the store and got groceries and it was so good that I almost passed out.

We barreled down island roads and screamed in each other's faces, "I want a man who can say beautiful things. I don't want to go out with anyone who says *my condo* instead of *my apartment!*" One of them referred to a man we know as "a ham sitting in hot ham water and the water is getting cooler and he is just the wet pink pork." We were on vacation! We looked at our normal lives and at some of the letdowns and we just cut the fat for each other. Nobody in that car needed to worry about a pot of hot ham water. We made that clear and final and we just left it in the dust.

It was the early afternoon and the day had been too chilly for outright swimming, but it had been perfect for being outside. We walked to a small beach. On the beach, we talked about our art and some bad boyfriends and sex and then nice boyfriends and how we felt about horseshoe crabs. I looked at the jellyfish while another woman looked out at the ocean and was so obviously full of her own useful inner combat that it seemed like she could have thrown her head into the sea as some sort of challenge. The third woman was somewhere farther down the cove, squatting over something that had washed up, laughing to herself.

The planet itself saw us. I saw it see us, I think. I think it saw us while we were doing exactly what we wanted, and then it was happy. I watched my friends walk around on the sand. I would look up over the top of my book and see a woman pop up in the water. I would crane my neck to look behind me and one of them would be using an old camera to take a picture of my butt. The three of us were intensely bright in our desire for each other's adoration and gaze, and in our appetites to be set free as a small roving herd.

I could feel it but I didn't want to say it out loud because my friends were new friends and they were younger than me—so maybe this freedom and wildness was how they always felt and lived and I was just kind of a repressed dorky square—but either way, I felt us all slip out of and step right over a shroud of rules that often drapes me in a fine chainmail of *oh no you don't.*

Whatever usually fundamentally restrains me just evaporated like mist in our good heat.

We didn't need to have shirts on or any clothes that we didn't want. A rabbit doesn't have socks. Why would a woman have a bra if she was making a snack in her natural habitat, which is of course a house by the sea? We put our groceries away in states of undress, we drank beer while making cocktails. We got in the bathtub together and sat there like toddlers, like psychic siblings, like little clams. We took a three-hour bath, getting in and out to bring in new treats. Somebody took a nap during the bath. We let the cold go down and kept putting in the warm when we needed it. We kept cups of wine around the tub.

In the night, we slept restlessly but it wasn't a problem because most of what we were doing in the day was draping ourselves over everything in the world and then drifting off. At night, we put on lipstick and took a pill and rode a taxi for thirty-five minutes into town so that we could chomp lamb chops and caviar in a very old and charming restaurant filled with stiffs and spinsters. We took our picture in front of the fireplace like three lieutenants from an army of dazzling women, here on earth to gallop through your beach house and make you feel crazy, baby!

One night, we roasted a chicken and had our chests bare and we ripped that hot chicken apart with our wicked little hands—we didn't even wait for plates. We didn't even think about plates. We were honest-to-god female animals with each other and I felt that, because of how we floored it like that, we could be animals with the other animals, too. I saw it clearly: One woman could go outside and sit on a rock and a fox could come and sit next to her and put its paw on her back the way a buddy does to encourage another buddy or to apologize for losing a temper. They would look at the sunset together, sniff the air, make a plan to meet up later on and howl. I would look out the window while shaking a colander of tomatoes and see her shaking the fox's paw and saying, "Nice to meet you. I'm Mae," and I'd watch the fox trotting off and calling out, "See you later for the howl!"

One of us could just drop off the deck, flipping backwards onto the back of an osprey. She would take a flight down the beach and back while the other two of us chopped carrots. "Where's Jane?" "Oh, she's on that bird right now—I think I just saw them circle the lighthouse." "Oh, okay. Do we want white wine with this? If so, we're going to have to put an ice cube in because I forgot to stick it in the fridge. I'm having beer now anyway. When she's back from the bird-ride we will ask her to do the potatoes."

As for me, I would be allowed to kiss a rabbit. Not for a sex need, just for sweetness between two creatures, just to be allowed to be seen as a fellow animal and not a predator, just for touching the untouchable . . . that would be my special delight.

I would see the rabbit on the lawn by the back door and I would put down my vegetable peeler and wipe my hands on my pants. "Hi," I'd say quite plainly, swinging open the screen door. My feet would go from the steps onto the grass and clover. The rabbit would peek up at me and not be afraid of me at all. I'd have my pants on but absolutely no top and I'd raise the rabbit up and feel its soft stomach and its paws on my chest. Its back feet would press into the top of my breasts as it climbed toward my face but it wouldn't scratch my skin or put any bugs on me.

The rabbit would smell my chin and it would push a paw into my cheek to try to see what I was. Then I would angle my head down and feel the two hot tufts of air push out from the little nose of the animal. I would blow my own two air tufts and see the fur move on the crown of its head. The rabbit would press its forehead against my mouth for a kiss. I would kiss its little head and press back with my mouth, and then the rabbit would flip its face up and kiss me one small kiss, right on the lips, anointing me into the real animal realm, one paw now pressing into the space between my nose and eye, where tears track sometimes. I would be able to smell the woods on the rabbit and it would smell roses and beer on me.

I would stick my tongue out like when you are trying to catch a snowflake and the rabbit would stick its tongue out too and press the delicate pink petal-tongue into my own tongue, like a stamp. Then eventually when I would speak again, all of the words would pass over my stamped tongue, and whatever I'd say would be marked by the rabbit stamp of acceptance that says, "I am a gentle creature. You can listen to me completely because I am not trying to hurt anything."

Then the rabbit would make a noise that I have never heard before, and it would kiss my jaw, and it would kiss me right below the ear, and then it would climb onto my shoulder, and pull my necklace with its paw. It would want my necklace so that it could be like me. I would think about it and then take off the necklace with the little J on it, and put it around the rabbit's torso like a sash. The rabbit would be proud and leap off my shoulder, bounding into the woods to show the other animals what it had.

When I'd come inside, my friends would be sitting on the floor, putting wood in the fireplace. "Who was that?" they'd ask. "It was a rabbit," I'd say.

We all fell asleep watching a movie in my bed. We cried and ate potato chips. We got more than a glimpse of what we could be if there were no boundaries for us, no world but this. Because of these two women who brought a boatload of love to me on a small island, I eventually stopped wondering thoughts like, "But what if hot ham water could turn into a love potion?"

I started to understand how to move away from near-misses with dead pink meat and into the live animal world, getting wild and gentle kisses from better animals. Instead of asking the old questions that sounded like "What is wrong with me?" I would start asking important questions like "What if I only dreamed gardens, what if I ate carrots because what if I were a pleasant rabbit? What if I got a crown for doing nothing but being who I am, what if even just one plant said hi to me or a tree bashfully bowed as I walked by, what if my dog knew what I meant when I wave to him? What if I could always be a little bit on this island in my mind? What if I could always be a little bit naked, a little bit kissing everything, an unplundered trove of my own love?"

A Prayer

As the image of myself becomes sharper in my brain and more precious, I feel less afraid that someone else will erase me by denying me love.

I Was Born: About to Bust

I was born on the boundary line between cold and hot, at the intersection of the two elements that make a clap of thunder.

I was born at the time of year when the sun wants to warm the earth but the winter has frozen it almost to the point of permanent frigidity. I was born when living things remember to wake up again. I was born just when you think that birth won't happen, because it has been cold for so long.

* * *

I was born on March 25, at the outermost reaches of winter, between the end of cold and the beginning of thaw that spreads out into warmth and richness that both is inevitable and requires patience.

I was born at exactly the time when anything alive is saying, "LET. ME. BURST! Let me get to the most beautiful and ornamental and essential version of what I can be. Give me space to bloom and present the blossoms to an ecosystem that will drink from my nectar, celebrate my petals, sniff me, pick me, take me home, make your body smell like my lovely scent." I was born during the moment in the cycle when almost every single live thing is inclined to mate, to grow, to point a snout skyward and sniff the air, to create.

In the very grooves of my being is the desire to bust open, and the certainty that it is right to begin to live again even after long periods of cold and darkness.

I was born a hospital baby in Boston, Massachusetts, at 11:17 AM, and I was choking on the cord that connected me to my mother. I was born and the first thing that happened was that I was made free to live. Then I was loud. Then I never wanted to go to sleep.

* * *

I was born and I was a baby and right then, the crocuses were trying to come up and there was still snow.

I grew up a little bit and I tromped through still frozen woods and I would see the little crocuses pushing up and I would be so thrilled to see them, and so achingly worried about their survival, about them *being killed,* or not having the hardiness to live through the night. It always seemed that the crocuses did not know what was best for them, that they had put their heads up too early, that they were too fragile and wouldn't admit it, and that they had come up when it was still dangerous.

Are they forcing it? No, somebody always needs to go first. I know this. I go first.

I was born in the time when crocuses show that they are holy because they are fragile but excited to pop up and they are brave enough to wave the flag of the change of season. There is a recklessness to that thrusting up. I contain that in spades, as they say.

A few weeks after I was born, the apple blossoms exploded with sleeves and sleeves of perfect pinks and there were wild daffodils in the woods, sprouting as trios, and pond-shaped areas of lily-of-the-valley that smelled so good that it would maybe almost hurt me because of how much I wanted them to be there.

The pretty things gathered to live just as I arrived.

We would cut whole apple blossom branches off and bring them inside. Bring that wildness into the house! That billowing fragrance, bring it in on fragile boughs with green inside of them under that thin bark!

I was born and everything in nature seemed like arms reaching out. I was born and the wildness from outside put itself inside of me. That wildness was my first baby spirit food. I sipped it right down before I drank milk from my mother.

These are the events that put their sequence in my bloodstream, and so I am a creature of this realm that rushes up and out, at the start of the spring.

Nice Things to Do for Tipping Yourself Toward Gentleness and Simple Joy

Go for a walk outside.

While you are on the walk, if there is a person with a dog, look at the dog and say, "Hi!" Say hi to the dog first. And then look up at the person and laugh—a small three-bubble laugh—and say, "Hi," kindly, as if they know that their dog is great and you know it too, as if it's normal to say hello to the dog before hello to the person, as if it is normal to say hello to a dog at all, as if the person and you understand something together. You don't have to decide what that thing is. It's about the feeling and the feeling will most likely be there, and the experience begins and ends with that.

Put on very fancy classical music and make yourself sit still and listen to it. Say the names of the different instruments to yourself in your head. Horn. Violin. Harp. Cymbal, baby! Now, of course imagine the orchestra and the instruments and use what energy you have left to imagine different animals playing the instruments. Break a few rules. For example, if you want, a horse can be sitting in a chair or playing an instrument that obviously requires fingers. It doesn't matter. It's fake. But the feelings that you will have when you think of the thing will be real feelings.

Write a note of encouragement to yourself and put it in a drawer that you use a lot. Later in the day, when you go to get a spoon or a sweater, there it will be, looking up at you, saying something like "You are a little sweetheart, aren't you?" or something like that. It will be good to feel a little embarrassed by the heightened emotion of the note. It will be good to have a treat and a non-gross secret like this note.

* * *

Clean a room and tidy it with an air of fairness, like you are doing what is fair for the room. Say something like "There you are, now," to the room when you are done fussing over it. Sit in the room for at least a few minutes and listen and do that and only that, which is actually hard and different than spacing out. It is hard to sit still and listen to everything you can listen to on purpose.

If there is an animal to hold and soothe or just smooth the fur, do that.

Turn your head to the side and give yourself a little kiss on the shoulder.

Wash your face and hands.

Put on an outfit of all one color.

Only do a little gossip and make sure it doesn't make any dents in anyone.

I Died: The Sad Songs of My Vagina

Oh, somebody write a letter to someone else, please!
Let them know that I'm dead now because I died.
Before I totally died, I was fatally ill.

Symptoms: I'd started to fall down all of the stairs
every time I tried to descend. Something was saying,
*There's no point in trying anymore. Just get down to the
bottom. Just be a heap.*

Also my clothes kept flying off me.

I would be in a store, buying a small wooden animal
for my mantel, and suddenly my pants and underpants

93

would rip right off. They would frantically flap away, always in the same direction. My pants and underpants, as if yanked on a line from someone as strong as Poseidon, knocked things off shelves and smashed through the glass in the window of the store and there I would be, revealed as a terminally ill woman with both bare butt and vagina. I would also get stuck with a large bill for the damage to the merchandise and the structure of the store itself.

If it were just a table clock or a vase, we would absorb the cost, especially considering your condition, Ms. Slate, they would explain meekly, as I stood there still holding a wooden fox and choosing to cover my vagina with both hands and fox. My bare butt cheeks were greeting new customers.

We're a small business and the cost of the window is just more than we can take on.

I totally understand, I would say, with a kind smile that showed an endearing glimpse at my humiliation without making the shopkeeper feel my actual despair or pain. I would still buy whatever thing I was holding, even if it was something that I had just grabbed because it was falling off a shelf.

Other symptoms: My bush turned light pink.

My nipples grew diamonds right in the center of the center.

My vagina started singing only the sad songs from a jukebox in my childhood home, a jukebox that I would listen to as a young girl and then imagine falling in love, a jukebox as big as a refrigerator. It was big. Love seemed big too, like an elephant that you can have if you are good.

My vagina never sang the Andrews Sisters, like it could have. It didn't even croon out any Perry Como. It was just Jo Stafford "Keep It a Secret" and sometimes it sang "Ghost Town" in a minor key, with a lot of snark. My hair became thousands of strands of fine golden necklaces and they got tangled all of the time and they made little cuts and chafes on the back of my neck, on the soft skin of my back. Little red slits on my delicate shoulder blades.

My disease was rotting me, but more quickly than rot usually happens. That was because I was suffering from supplemental illnesses that came on when my immune system got weak:

Heart-worm, wish-rot, brain-foam, butt-sag.

I had taken to my bed. I was a grand little dame, so young still, such a shame. I was lying in my bed and I was wearing very beautiful pajamas. Oh, isn't it just too desperately sad?

I was dying of a disease but I was never in a snit about

it. I was so nice still, and everyone was coming in to see me. They craned their necks at the door.

"Hi, boo-boo," said my friends, walking in softly like the floor was made of a thin layer of that sugar glass that they use to break over people's heads in jokes on TV.

My sheets were crisp. No nail polish, just clean hands. I wasn't covered in sores, nor was I unsightly because of cracks in the epidermis. I didn't suddenly have wiry hairs growing out of my face like you sometimes see when it all goes to shit. I didn't leak. Proximity to death never meant that I compromised my dedication to being chic and elegant.

I was a pro at dying. I bore it with dignity and grace and light jokes. The jokes were clear and weightless. They did not drag anyone into my pain. Nobody got a whiff of anything.

And then the moment was there. I started to formally pass away.

My friends came into the room. I was very accomodating. I took the death rattle wholly into myself, like when you shush people before a play. If you got close it just sounded like someone was jingling nickels and dimes and maybe plastic buttons in a velvet bag, somewhere else.

My friends were all around me. They stood closer than shoulder to shoulder. They smushed into each other. They broke the rules of personal space just to be in my bedroom and say goodbye to me. They bawled. They cried tears the size of dumplings. They felt each other shake.

They looked at my face. My weak little peepers opened up just a bit. I saw that they had broken their own rules for how close to be to other people. I saw that it was possible to do it, to be closer than is allowed. Maybe I never got it for myself, that kind of closeness during which emotion fuses you together and you can only see that there is a separation between you and your beloved if you use a microscope. Maybe I never got it for myself but I did see it for myself. I saw it with my dying eyes.

Colors started to ascend in a wave, right out of my body. They got clearer and more concentrated. My colors became the nice easy shapes that babies learn. There were triangles and squares floating in the air. There were at least five hundred circles. There were shafts of color pirouetting during my death. There were random blasts of colors with no shape but the sounds of French horns and bicycle bells and forks on wineglasses when they announce a toast.

A swarm of small lights came out of the tips of my fingers and toes and they sounded like crickets in the night. Each little pill of light in the swarm had wings but no face.

The whole room shimmied with the sound of the xylophone, drowning out the sad songs of my vagina.

Bing. Bong. Bing, plinked the xylophone in the lights and shapes and air.

I knew it: *That is my sound.* It was like a doorbell that rings, but so I can open a door to leave, not bring anyone in. I was my own guest and host at once at the end of my world.

I heard the sound of the bing-bong, and the electromagnetic field around my heart blushed maraschino cherry red. As my eyes fluttered and closed for good, the lights behind them blinked purple red purple and the blinks sounded a plunk and a fizz and everyone couldn't help but laugh at those goof-noises, like how babies laugh at sneezes.

The room went black, even though it was only the late afternoon. Then it was very quiet.

Write a letter to someone. Tell them that this is not a tragedy. The rest of me went home to the universe.

There is a rumor that I vroomed out of town on a red maraschino cherry with a wagging tail.

Mouse House

Hello, have you met me? I am a Mouse.

In the mornings of my life, I wake up and I blink my eyes open and I stretch my body with a shudder that holds tension like a string pulled so tight that it makes a musical sound when you pluck it with one finger.

When I wake up my body reacts so immediately to a new day that you can hear one high, bright note. I am so tuned to being alive that if you touch me it makes music.

* * *

My love is the first one who may hear that private sound. My love is a sexy rabbit. His heart beats in such strong thumps and his heart sounds like, far away, a wild boy is dribbling a hard ball all alone, practicing so that he can be the best, by his own standards. An earnest dribble. Full focus. My love has a heart beat and heart bounce just like me even though he is a different animal, and that's that.

I love to smell morning air and I always do. I love to walk quietly through my small mouse house. My feet are clean and rather long and my butt is a soft little pumpkin-rump and my tail is a chestnut-brown treble clef but yes I am a mouse. This is just how I name my parts because it is very pleasing to me to adorn myself with descriptions that I wear like clothes.

The floor is dry dirt that is packed down so that it is not dusty in here. I walk through my mouse house every early morning and I look at all of my own things, like my small table and my windowpanes and my acorn that I keep just for decoration. I walk through each bashful morning with renewed pride, and my heart is perky and smart as I open the door so that I can put myself into the world.

* * *

I step out into the sun and air and globes of dew. I can hardly take it, how full I am that there is a new day to have. And there right outside of my house, I have made a little flag for me, to signify that I live on my own personal land. Every time I see that it still stands and has not been trampled in the night, I drop open my tiny little mouth and sing out a victory note because there it is, a flag made of twig and blossom and leaf.

Holding the Dog

I stand in the middle of a room in the daytime when I should be doing a number of things, enough things to fill a list, but I do not do any of the things, I only stand in the middle of a room in a hotel filled with people who (I imagine) have un-ruined hearts. I stand there so still and look out the window and all I can think is maybe I will see your dog and all I can think is a made-up story: "I am on the street and the dog breaks free of you and free of your hold, and the dog runs away from you but I catch it." And while I'm putting this together in my mind I think, "But isn't the dog very strong and rather wiggly? I could never hold it." But I let myself have my thinking again, make the image, and in the image I hold on. I hold on to the dog and you come running up, sort of stressed but not as much as anyone should be when something runs away from them, because the crazy thing about you is that in almost every way you are an example of limits. And then the fantasy starts to melt or have an invisible morphing energy like flubby, distorted sound. I try to hold on. What should I be? I suppose I want to be the hero, but not really, and I want to be the one, but not really, anymore. Mostly I want you to look at me and realize what happened and say sorry at least, and really consider me for a moment in your own padded organized mind and then let me give you your dog back and I will take that tiny chunk of my identity back, the one that you walked off with, and I will take it back and hold on. And then you will just actually dissipate right there on the sidewalk and the dog will somehow be fine and I will stand up and maybe even have no memory of this whole thing, or just a vague memory of holding a loving dog in place for a moment on a street in another world.

I Died: Bonked

Well, let's see. This one is fun but also serious.

I got bonked on the head by a zig of lightning, and then I died.

But then somebody put my body in the ocean and I got yoinked around by the waves and that helped to get the gloop going inside of me and so I was born anew and I was alive again and I'd really only missed a few minutes of the world. But still, I felt shy and different. And then I glugged up out of the sea and onto the beach and a Big Sweetie blinked at me and even though I was shy, my clothes whipped themselves into a bikini and he blinked at me again and I knew my bikini would just woosh off completely if he blasted one more blink from his peepers, and I was so jumpy about the idea of what *that* would do that the pumper in my heart konked out and I died again!

Darnit. I was so close to being clasped by him! Timing is everything, little one.

But, listen, right when I died a good zag of lightning was zooming through the sky and it saw what had happened—that I had died from being eager to use my heart and get my body touched—and it decided to blow its last charge on me so that I could have what I hoped, and so the bolt bombed down and bonked me just like the other one did before and I sat right up in the sand and the Big Sweetie was blinking at me because I was a four-time miracle of dying and living and he said, "Do you think you're well enough for a dunk?" And I said, "I could probably manage a little dip," and so we splashed into the sea, and that's the story of how I met your grandfather. And we fell in love and we were together for a long time but it only felt like a zip, because that's what true love feels like. And we saw the sun and sipped our coffee together every single morning with our legs all tangled up under the sheets and we snoozed together every night and were each other's only boo-boo until the day that he croaked.

The Pits

I'm always picking at things when I am nervous or working up a real lather in my thoughts.

I'd gone to town on my fingers and I wasn't about to bite off my lips or fuck with my feet, so I went ahead and peeled the rind off my heart. Then I sort of ripped it apart and down to nothing, and I looked at what was there and I said factually, *This is the pits.*

The pits are also the seeds. The pit is also a deep place with an actual bottom. You could argue that the bottom of the pit is where you plant the start of the thing that is made to travel to the light. You could prove, if you tried to or wanted to, that the bottom of the pit is of course the start of getting up to the top.

But it is the planting of the pit that is the hard part. The part where you have to go down there and cover a small hard thing with dark matter. The part where you are supposed to believe in a process and the part when you must admit to your desire for the thing to work, and that is hard too. But you can do it if you want to try to do it, and the act is singular and special even though also you may have to do it many times over and a few of those times the pit will simply stay a pit. You will have to be comfortable with the truth that there is a stone in the dark, a grave for a hope. But if you can get a better view of what is going on, you can see that the problematic pit is really just a small hole along the path that is otherwise lined with the other living things that shot up toward the light.

To Norway

I got on the plane and I went from Los Angeles to Norway.

Every time I'm in an airport alone I have to remind myself that I am neither an orphan nor a plain virgin governess on her way to be insulted by the competitive and haughty family of her disagreeable ward.

In an airport in Norway, I was alone and looking at the different candies and snack foods. This is one of my favorite things to do in other countries. Also, I love being alone in airports and sitting at the bar and drinking a pint of beer. I do not get glasses of wine because that seems sad to me and even when I am happy, it sometimes happens that the slightest things can tip me into nonspecific sadness when I am alone. A glass of white wine would be devastating, for example, if I were alone. That's the kind of thing that would make me feel—again, for example—very divorced.

A pint of beer just keeps everything steady. Hello, I am just a beer drinker, in neutral transit.

I was drinking my beer and I saw a business lady buying a hot dog, and she was doing this in her business outfit and it was normal to her. In the USA, a businesswoman would not feel so free or dispassionate about buying a hot dog in an airport. I can't really imagine an American businesswoman doing this without imagining her either laughing or crying about it. Her hot dog purchase would be *a sign* of something *going on* with her. This Norwegian woman was just having lunch.

I thought that this was good news about what it might be like here in Norway, in terms of what this culture is and how the people are existing within it. They are eating what they like and doing their different works. No big deal about being an adult who is eating a hot dog in the middle of the day like a kid at a birthday party on a weekend. Here, it is hot dog on Wednesday in your midforties and there is nothing to even say about that but "Of course?"

On my connecting flight, there was a young baby with a huge bag of potato chips. The bag was as big as the body of the baby, and the baby would not let go of the bag even though its mother was trying to help it bear the burden of such a large parcel. The baby wanted to hold the bag but also it was thirsty. The baby spoke Norwegian to its mother and must have said in baby-Norse that it was thirsty, and so the mother got a drink out and the baby started drinking water through a straw and saying "Ahhhh" with great satisfaction.

The baby did not know that when I was a little girl in the eighties and nineties I used to take big gulps of drinks and say "AHHHH" as a joke, to my sisters or friends. The baby didn't know that I used to be a baby, somewhere else, but because I saw this baby I sort of knew it anew, that I had been a baby too.

* * *

There was a farmer on the airplane in the row behind me. He was talking to a stranger about how he was a farmer. Once we were in the air, the pilot got on the intercom and wished a sixteen-year-old boy a happy birthday, saying to this boy and all of the passengers that he hoped the birthday boy would "get lots of presents."

And then, because it was the thing to do, I prepared to sleep, fully clothed and sitting up next to a stranger while we shot through the evening sky.

In the town of Bergen, where I stayed for the night by myself, there were raincoats for sale in the window. It wasn't raining and the way they were displayed seemed like a straightforward and warmhearted suggestion. It felt like the raincoats said, "As a matter of fact, people are warmhearted, just as they are air breathers and leg walkers and eye see-ers. But sometimes rain makes them get all wet, and so here are coats in case that happens. They are reasonably priced and well made."

I went to where my friend told me to go to eat dinner and I let spaghetti hang out of my mouth while I was alone in the restaurant. I didn't let it hang for a long time, I just paused for a moment and noticed that the pause made me feel embarrassed, not the noodle.

Then, it's hard to describe how happy the breakfast at the little hotel made me feel. It wasn't because it was a huge spread, although it was certainly not skimpy. It was the combination of the offerings. It was that there was pickled fish but also cherry jam. The bread was yellow. There was ham but also cucumbers were sliced and arranged nicely. The yogurt was thin and tart and the coffee was splendid.

The night before, the man in the room next to me snored loudly, but I wasn't cross at all. And yes, the word to use is *cross,* but again, I wasn't at all. It is so nice to be a little bit closer to other humans. No soundproofing or blocking when a hotel is just a big old mansion from three hundred years ago. It is nice to be with strangers, and everyone is trying to sleep, and we are all in nothing but a big old house. The facts are enough. And then the breakfast just pushed it all over the edge.

I found my way to the docks so that I could take the two-hour ferry to where my friend and her sweetheart were waiting for me. They were with two other women as well. They were all friends. I was really only friends with *my* friend and I was new and I was shy and so of course I was also very brave. For the fjord boat, a man brought for himself a bottle of pink wine, a long sandwich, and a small can of pineapples.

The can of pineapples was a cousin to the airport hot dog.

On the ferry, I noticed that there was an upside-down dent in the clouds that looked like a hole to something else, like a funnel to an upside-down kingdom, for example. A seagull was in the water, trying to push ahead. The wind spun him around so that his butt was facing where he was trying to go. His expression was still the same, even though his face was where his butt should have been and his butt was facing his destination. He showed no signs of stress.

A grumpy young man was the ticket person on this boat. He was also the person in charge of running the little snack bar. The boat moved from its dock so quickly that it seemed like it was controlled by his mind or his expression, like how somebody gets their horse to start going just by nodding at it, not that I really know about that because I dislike horses and have refused to know the truth about them and how they work.

I listened to music and I watched what passed and I saw animals on the piney islands and I didn't know if they were small goats or large cats, but of course large cats are not the right answer.

When I arrived at the town and met my party of new friends, we went to dinner in a castle named after a woman called Karen. Karen was from the 1600s but her name was Karen. I have never had a really great feeling about castles because I don't love the image of old kings. Old kings in the past are always dying of wet coughs and flaking faces, while being propped up on a million dirty velvet pillows. I find those images to be disgusting, but that was not what this castle was like. It was lovely and cozy and good.

Inside of the castle, there were many geraniums on the windowsills, in two colors, red and pale pink. I was making a normal face but because of those geraniums, nothing inside of me was normal because it was just all fresh air in there, just possibility, no bones or muscles or anything else. I love red geraniums.

* * *

I took a walk and there was a young Norwegian teen by a very old barn. He was doing a waltzy hip-hop dance while eating an ice cream cone.

The next day, we played cards, walked through gardens, smelled every flower, got drunk, ate a lot of halloumi cheese, and one night I ordered from the children's menu while I sat at the table with my adult friends. I ordered from the children's menu because it had a dish called "Sausages" and I wanted that more than the more traditional, fish-based fare on the main menu.

When my dinner arrived, it was a plate and on the plate were two long, curved, naked hot dogs. The waitress seemed angry to have to give it to me. Although I was not attempting to recreate the soothing normal hot dog situation that I saw with the businesswoman in the airport, I was aware that I was not even close to accomplishing whatever she had accomplished. I was a bit embarrassed of my weiners but I still ate them and they were fine. None of my new friends cared.

When I went farther up into the Arctic Circle with my friend and her sweetheart, we met another friend of theirs. He was tall and had dark hair and I enjoyed talking to him but I could never really look him in the eye for a number of reasons. He made an apple pie, roasted a chicken, drove the car, painted me a picture of a small blue flower, and said my name when calling me over to look at a horse that he knew I was not happy about. He told me lines from a poem that he heard in a dream.

We all went out in a boat and we were rowing from the house to a little island with a lighthouse on it. When we were halfway there, we realized that it was much farther than it had seemed when we were standing on our own shore, but we made it there and when we got there the island was covered in gorgeous shells and the lighthouse was actually strangely small, like a nub. We sat there and my friend realized that she'd forgotten the wine and when she realized she forgot the wine, she stuck her tongue out in embarrassment. I just loved her so much and I always will and I remembered that I'd seen her stick her tongue out like this previously, when we had crashed our sleds the winter before, also, strangely, in Norway.

Later, while my friend and I sat upstairs in the house we were staying in, her sweetheart and the dark-haired man went outside in the Arctic midnight sun and went skinny-dipping in the ocean. I watched him go in. "That's his butt," I said to my friend. "Yes," she said seriously, "that's his butt." Then the next day I had to go home because that had been the plan. I said goodbye to all of them and I felt very odd. Something had happened but nothing had happened, really. Nobody touched me but it felt like I had been touched.

On the way home to the United States, a man on the plane spilled his coffee on his seat. He got up and showed it to the flight attendant, and he pointed at the spill with a smile that was shy but also had a little light in it like he was thinking of a funny memory but knew it would make no sense to anyone else if he were to laugh into the air of the plane. She wasn't mad at him and understood that he didn't want to sit in the coffee puddle, and they figured out how to deal with it.

Across from me, a girl with a silver sparkly scrunchie was looking at pictures, and even though I was far away and I couldn't make out the face in the pictures, I could tell that it was her in the pictures because the person in the pictures also had a silver scrunchie. I really liked her for looking at her pictures of herself.

* * *

I cried a lot on the airplane home, come to think of it.
My life was not in place. Many things had jabbed at me
during my trip. I was affected by seeing how other people lived and what they thought was normal. In my own
life, a lot actually seemed off. I wanted things to be as
easy as when I saw the lady buy the hot dog. I wanted
things to be as satisfying as the baby with the big bag of
chips and the sips of a drink that made it say "Ahhhh."

I thought about how I could not bring my eyes to meet
the man who painted the blue flower.

I looked into my heart for the first time in a long time
and I saw a door to something. I thought my heart had
been close but it had been farther than I thought, like
when we went to the island and it was not as near as it
seemed. But we got there. I thought about how I was
wanting to get to my heart and wondering what shells
it had all over it, what things lay ready for discovery for
me and someone else. Or would I just be a nubby lighthouse saying "Don't crash!" to other people who were
only passing by? I thought about it on the plane, and
about how I'd had my eyes cast down on the trip but I'd
still seen a butt, and then I was on the plane and I was
crying too hard on the plane.

* * *

I tried to write down how I felt. I recently found the note I wrote to myself, and all it said was "I'm too overwhelmed to say any more and I'm too scared to say any more and I feel too foolish, but I must not forget this, so I'm writing this down and this is the best that I can do."

Hillside

My house was built in 1912, which is so very long ago that I imagine the house was born as a tree and then grew wider and higher and breathed in so much air that it made pockets in the wood, pockets like caves that then made themselves into rooms with hard corners and floors.

The house was born as a tree because that's just the fact. The fact is that my house was born as many trees, and the trees lived for so long and had roots in deep dark brown earth. They had their own barks all over themselves. Animals climbed all over them too.

* * *

They were part of a forest, an ecosystem that is perfect because of its wide variety of species, dominant because nothing is *not allowed* to be there. In the forest, everything that is inclined to thrive really does, and has a job, and some jobs are to grow things up and some jobs are to take things apart and everything is accepted because there is no notion—among bacteria and moss and busy mice—there is no notion of who deserves to do something or be in a place. There are only lives to be lived, and they are everywhere.

That's where my house was born. It was born as a million billion small medium and large live things, and then someone came and got some of those many live things and made them into pieces of an anticipated whole and then that all became my house. And for over a hundred years, people lived in the house. I don't know who died here, or how many people might have been here at once, sleeping in the rooms. I don't know what soups might have been made in the kitchen, or if there were ever robbers or maybe a surprise party, or where the sex happened, or if there were things like a bird in a birdcage or a piano in the living room.

* * *

The house is on a steep hill, but I don't have a view that looks out and down, like most people want to have. The road that I live on is a notch in the hill, like a part in a hairstyle. It is just a ridge in a slope. I have a front porch and for over a hundred years it has been looking across at the rest of the hill, and the hill rises right up in front of your eyes. It is covered in wild vines and bushes and cactuses and bougainvillea. There is a bedroom on the second floor of the house, right above the porch. It has very large and of course very old windows. If you stand in the hall and look through the room and right out the window, all you see is different greens, the wild ropes of leaves and the bends of willowy plant life, everything bowing, braiding, climbing on each other. You stand in my house and see a green overgrowth of ivy and saplings and flowers and eucalyptuses that, when they are wet or moved, sigh out with a minty blue fragrance.

I bought this house for myself and my small old dog. I bought it during the one trillionth time that I've had my heart broken. I saw that someone had carved initials in the basement floor in 1969. I had heard that an old man had shown up here, walked into the kitchen, pointed to the refrigerator, and said, "Why is that not the stairs?"

He told the real estate agent that this had been his grand-parents' house. What were all these people doing here?

On a Sunday afternoon, I went outside in my slippers and picked my kumquats from two young, slight trees. I picked ten Meyer lemons and five oranges. I picked yellow Mexican marigolds that smelled so strong, and all I could hear was the air moving the plants, and what I could smell was the perfume of the marigolds on my hands mixed with the wild lemon and orange scents. It was quiet and peaceful and I spoke out loud to the mystery of people, to the traces of the lives that had lived here before me. I imagined them looking out at me from the kitchen windows as I pulled up my sweatshirt to use it as a basket for the fruit. I grinned and showed my bare abdomen to my house and dog, and filled my sweatshirt with oranges.

I imagined a ghost of an actress from the thirties, a young woman filled with life and bitterness, who called nail polish "varnish." I imagined her looking at me and all of the oranges and my stomach and saying, "She's gonna bring all of *that* into *here?*"

And I do bring all of that into here—that's kind of the main thing I do in every situation. Like it or not, I bring it into the here and now. But the other thing is that I keep a pretty keen eye on everything that has gone into making whatever "here" is, like the trees and the lives.

I feel very lonely sometimes, and I felt very lonely when I bought the house. But I walk through the back door into the kitchen and I say to the oranges that they have made me the happiest woman on earth, and I say to however many ghosts might be watching me that I am so glad to be in the house, and I let my loneliness be there too, here in a very old house in a notch in a living hillside, not looking out and down but looking straight into the energetic wildness that drapes itself all over itself and has many mysterious roots that shoot deep into the earth.

Important Questions

I'm humble enough to admit that I don't know everything and I'm secure enough to ask questions.
Examples:

How can I shrink enough to be small enough to
respectfully ride a lamb or dachshund?
What would my body look like (specifically boobs,
butt, hair) if I only ate food cooked by bolts of
summer lightning?
What happens if I put a spell on a tiny piece of

paper, put that into a nectarine, and bury it?
What kind of tree could result from this action?
Does the violin know about the cricket? Has a
cricket ever lived in a violin?
What if, when I felt a little off, I could flip up the
top of my head and sprinkle just a few flowers
around my brain and then flip the top of my
head back down?
What if a moonbeam gets caught in my soup and I
swallow it in a sip and then I always float a little
bit off the ground because there is a moonbeam
in my stomach?
Can I wrestle on the lawn? Can I sleep on the
lawn? Who invented lawns?
Who is more chatty, a squirrel or a seagull?
When I die, will I turn into a ghost or just be
garbage until I am part of a garden?

I Died: Sardines

I died! Do you know? And can you believe it?

I was in the kitchen with my father, on a Friday afternoon at maybe a little bit before four PM, and I opened
a circular tin of sardines and furthermore I knew that
there was a lemon in the refrigerator. These were the
conditions. And I opened the tin of sardines very care-
fully so as not to spill the oil, and there they all were in
there, perfectly nestled into each other, these plump, oily,
salty little fishes. There they all were and I knew that I
was about to make a sandwich for my father and that

I was a lucky person and I saw it so completely and I will tell you what: I just died. I simply passed right away. By the time I went to get the lemon I was only a spirit. By the time I laid the little guys on the toast, the soft spines still in their bodies, the bread drenched in lemon juice, the whole thing dusted with fine black pepper, by the time I cut two fat fancy caperberries each in half and laid them on top of it all, I was nothing but a holy holy girl ghost. And when I gave my father his very own sandwich and it was much more exciting than he was expecting, I was a new saint. And when I opened my pretty mouth to chomp the little sardine bodies and the bread and the lemon juice and pops of pepper flecks and slips of caperberries, I blasted back into life with such essential joy that (good sweet goodness gracious!) I just about died again!

Sit?

I saw a little boy put his puppy on a skateboard and say "Patrick. Sit?"

There are a few things to say right away.

The first is that he wanted the dog to sit on the skateboard and not on the ground. What is that for? Why? The other first thing to say is how it makes me feel a sort of completeness that this young one has apparently named his dog Patrick. I wonder if the puppy is perhaps named after a character in a book or a movie, or maybe after a cousin who is admirable? The third (other "first") thing to say is that he said "Sit?" And not "Sit." He was not sure if it would work, or was uncomfortable with giving a command to the thing that is his friend and ward and companion. It is not natural to be a master in a casual way, to some of us. The last and only thing that I could say and that I mean with all of my heart is that I wish them both the best for all of the years that are coming to them as a pair of companions.

Kathleen/Dog-Flower-Face

I don't know who used to live here. Only I live here, me and the old dog.

I hired a woman named Kathleen to come and make a fence around my house so that I could be safe in a self-imposed pen, like an old goose or a young pig. Like both, really.

I hired her to start me a small garden of plants that would bloom throughout the year, so that there would always be a flower to say hello to when I return home. I was incredibly eager to tell her what plants I love and to make sure that she would not give me anything like an azalea or somehow misunderstand me and just roll up with a bunch of cactuses and gravel and make me look like a severe woman who has no idea what's going on. Having "no idea what's going on" is my central fear, most days.

I told her that I wanted people to come through the big garden door, into my pen, and feel a rush of wildness and color, and to encounter many different green forms. I wanted to present a big, full energy markedly different from the stress of whatever is outside my walls. I told her that I wanted my garden to be like the inside of what I see in myself. You see my garden, you come into my home, and it tells you not just what I like to see and what I want to be around, but how you should treat me. *I am the live thing that belongs here, with other live things like this.*

This is what I told the woman named Kathleen.

Kathleen patiently told me about the plants and flowers that could live in my garden. My small old dog walked with us and we looked at the sunlight and shade. I pointed to a bunchy blue burst of flowers growing on the hillside, sort of a vine that didn't lie flat, a bramble. The flowers looked like the shape of a fruit, and I always like it when those two images, fruits and flowers, gesture to each other. I like that and I always have, and I like it when fruit is in flower arrangements and I like it when flowers are in the salad or on cakes and I like it when fruits are on women's heads in their hats or if their whole hat is fruit.

I have always adored a cornucopia, of course.

I pointed at the blue hill-flowers and asked her, "Can I have that kind?" She told me that I could certainly have it. And then, very seriously, she said, "The only thing is that dogs love to smell the blossoms and they are actually very sticky, so your dog will have flowers on his face, and I don't know if you'd like that."

"I would like that," I told her.

What I didn't tell her was that when she asked me that question about flowers on my dog's face, she showed me that a legitimate option for experience— a true one that is real and is deeply concerned with beauty—could be mine. This was my home and my world and the future was all geared up and ready for pleasure and we were getting specific: Do you or do you not want flowers that stick to a dog's face? Yes or no? If yes, I was a citizen of the world of breezes and Sticky-Dog-Face-Flower. With every small choice, the world was emerging. What would I like, from all of it?

I didn't tell Kathleen how dear it was to me that

she told me this sticky-flower fact in total earnestness. I didn't tell her that even though everything about me really points to liking things like flowers on animals' faces, I was pleased that she did not assume. I was pleased that she made sure. Because in making sure, Kathleen gave me the opportunity to say out loud to another person that *I would like my old dog to have flowers stuck to his face,* and when I said it out loud—that yes, I would like that—I knew it was true. Then I admired myself. What's more, I felt tenderness about my personality and my choices for delight. I said who I was, on my land.

I didn't tell her that she was making me more than one garden. One outer, one inner. I was woozy as I watched a space open up inside of my inner me-garden, space that would be private just for me, in which I could observe myself and be private as I gazed upon myself.

I didn't tell her, "Hey, Kathleen? You've revealed yourself to be a woman of wonderful character." Rather than being unconsciously lazy and *telling me something,* she had reached out and grabbed a moment. No, she did not miss the moment, this woman Kathleen. She asked a question and so much bloomed and the plants weren't even there yet.

What I didn't say, because I selfishly wanted to keep the sweet sap of the moment swelling inside myself, undiluted, was "Actually, more than anything, I would like my dog to have small blue flowers stuck to his small face as often as possible, and now that you mention it, I want this more than most things that I want, but most of the things that I want are like this thing, and it is a *certain type of person* who feels this way that I feel, and I'm proud to be one, and now I see that I must really not forget that the style of what I find beautiful is incredible to me, that it is incredible to feel lucky to want to *want* what one wants, to be able to see the rings of yourself this way, and honestly, Kathleen, I am dead serious on this one."

Letter: Super-Ego

Dear Ms. Slate:

We were absolutely thrilled when, roughly three years ago, you got your hands on an Adam Phillips article in the *London Review of Books* about self-criticism and the super-ego. We were encouraged when you seemed to take in the information and hold it up to your own interior experience. We looked on in approval as you paraphrased the article to friends and strangers, telling them things like "The super-ego is reiterative. It repeats the most boring, pointy, hurtful things, and if you met it at a party, if it were a person, you would think that the person was not only mean and insane, but also not as smart as they think they are. You wouldn't listen. You would think they were a shithead."

You spent time passing this information around, yet upon close analysis, you did not seem to be passing it through yourself. It seemed to be lodged in your mouth, right in your little mouth, like an echo just bouncing around and then flying out of your face at parties and even in meetings, and then it would bounce off other people's faces and right back into your mouth. Of course, you could have swallowed it down, or explored its flavors. You could have let it work its way through you, but instead you did nothing with this information except to tell it to other people.

Oh, Ms. Slate, you do know that *telling people things* is not the same as *living by the principle of the things,* right?

Clearly you do not know. If you insist on peddling these psychological wares without sampling them yourself, if you insist on talking about things that you only know about in form but not in function, you will put this entire operation in jeopardy of looking like a fraud, and you will drag this whole initiative toward time-wasting and identity failure.

It is with deep regret that we inform you that you have been put on probation. You will no longer be able to access this subject matter in conversational form; nor will you be able to casually email it around. Be advised, should you try to speak about this article or sort of bat around this super-ego stuff in general, we have activated the emergency system, and there is no override.

If you are to open your mouth and then plan to say something like "The super-ego has very tight margins and doesn't allow for variance," while secretly listening to that actual super-ego voice inside of yourself, the system will be alerted and you will be supplied with an emergency sentence and you will find yourself saying things like "Summer is the warm time," or "Babies are the youngest ones we have," or "Horses are too big," or anything that is true but rather hazy-sounding.

We believe that choice builds strength, and so we have provided a list of approved chat items for you. As we grow more confident in your ability to not secretly shit on yourself all of the time, we shall expand the list. Our hope is that one day, you will not need this list at all, and will be able to speak freely and without the secret sibling of self-abuse and shaming.

But for now, your approved topics are as follows:

"I want to learn to be a better gardener," "Veal is a bummer and it's not even that good," "Library," "Baryshnikov: any and all performances/his face/his voice/him," "How to do bagels," "Swimming in the Atlantic Ocean," "Swimming in the Pacific Ocean," "Evergreen trees," "Why celery is not exactly what you wish," "Fits of bras," "Fits of jeans," "Caves," "Explain Easter?" "Paper cut stories," "Grandmothers," "Mustards of the world," "The astronaut who wore the diapers so that she didn't have to stop on her way to murder somebody," "Snowboarding: I can't try," "Aunts and their houses," "Ghosts, of course," "Going to the bathroom on the plane or the train," "Jars," "Maggots and mold," "Pumpkin carving," "Doritos," "Can a skunk be de-skunked and become a pet or will it be fundamentally gloomy without its stink?" and the follow-up "I love skunk smell, actually." Furthermore you may access themes around "Grapes," "Tropical fruits," "Volcano," "Cucumber," "*Sesame Street* in the past," "Wars," and "Gaudí was the One and Only and I love how he stuck fruits and shells into the holy structures he was inspired to create," "Monochromatic outfits," "New Year's resolutions," "Silk outfits," "Graves," "In *Peter Pan,* did you ever notice that the actor who plays the dad also usually plays Captain Hook? But not in *Hook* the movie," "Potluck dinners," "Swamps, marshes, and bogs," "What mushrooms do," "Acrimony," "Scoliosis," "Wells and buckets," and "The amazing Dukakis family."

We're aware that this list may seem limited but it simply mirrors the limits that you have shown to the community. Hopefully adherence to these guidelines will condition you to be able to take deeper dives on your own and become honest and free.

We look forward to watching your progress and growth. We yearn for it, even, Ms. Slate. We yearn for it. It is with faith and love that we say: It doesn't have to be this way. You don't need to do this anymore, and judging from what we caught you murmuring while you were on drugs by yourself at five in the morning, you know this to be true.

Sincerely yours,
The Office of Internal Affairs

Creed

Yes, it has been a long day and there have been strings of days recently, weeks, of empty and painful situations. There has been a rash of experiences that are empty and painful at once. There have been *only* empty times when there was no pain, only emptiness, and my body felt cold and dry and the sky looked white during the day and the night.

Then there were times that were *only* painful, during which I've lumbered through regret, humiliation, self-doubt, and feelings with loud blabbering blubbering voices that say, "Well, here it is. I'm the ugliest I've ever been," or "Well, this is it. This is how it starts. This is how it all starts. Watch, watch your career, relationships, and youthful physique just float away from you like trash in outer space. You've begun the docking process that signifies the start of terminal failure. And you, you brain-peasant, won't give up, so this whole thing is most likely going to last another seven years before you really admit it's even happening and then four years after that until you finally can see that the shape of your failure is final and hardly spectacular or unique. Here you are now. Nothing that happens now or after will count as much as anything you've done before."

Things like that. Yes, there have been lots of feelings that have felt like breaths in with no out breaths.

So, yes, it has been a hard time and nobody could say differently. But it occurs to me as this long day ends— and I can hardly make myself stay up past six PM because I'm too busted up in my heart, because my brain has the posture of an old couch, because I try to imagine the blood in my arms and all I can imagine is air being blasted through pipes made of paper . . . It occurs to me as I fight so hard with myself that these cruel and persistent voices are the echoes of trauma from the times when people treated me like I am now treating myself.

And that, perhaps, it is possible to close an inner door and shut out voices that are not mine. In the last light of a long day, I sit on a chair on my porch and watch the sky drain colors down and out and I realize I want to hear my voice and only mine. Not the voice of my voice within a cacophony of old pains. Just mine, now.

And then, at the end of this day, in the start of another night, at the first lip-lick of this appetite for hearing myself clearly, it really hits me: I never really want to argue with anyone ever again, nor am I under any sort of obligation to do so.

It occurs to me that I just never want to argue with a single person ever again and I will do anything I can to prevent it. Will I discuss? Yes. And will I disagree? Yes, I will also do that. I will also most likely feel classic lava-flows of anger.

But it is suddenly clear: I know what I want to hear when I hear myself in this life, and I am feeling very certain that there is absolutely no good reason to ever be disrespectful, no matter how upset you are. I do not need to hear bullying voices ever again and there is no reason to ever do that sort of emotional violence to anyone. There is no good rationale behind calling names or being tricky or cutting or scary or to say a ton of swears. That was never my style, but I let other people do it to me, and then I did something to them, too. And now, no.

I recall losing myself to eruptions of temper, and I deeply regret it all, and I regret it in a new way. It occurs to me that a rude and crude struggle is not anything that I can even connect to anymore.

It occurs to me, even as I'm not sure what's left of me, that I can use what is still alive to really behave in a way that I admire. It occurs to me that I can have every single feeling I need to have without ever trying to overpower someone or win something.

It occurs to me that if anyone is ever here again by my side I will do my best, and if that doesn't work out, I will leave. I will not do my half-best and stay for a ridiculous amount of time.

It occurs to me that if anyone ever bullies me again I will warn them one time but probably start to stop loving them, and that if they do it again I will have my final answer, that a person who does that to me does not love me. And then I will explain that their behavior has made it clear to me that I want to leave, and although I will have been clear, I will have been respectful, I will leave without participating in condemnation. I will go without digging deeper into the dark.

And then it occurs to me that it is never too late to

write yourself a good little personal creed, and that finding a creed for yourself is about gathering a set of rules that supports your self-respect and your community. It occurs to me that even though I feel very much at sea, I am noticing that I am finally mature enough to develop a creed and to live by it, and that this will no doubt cause me great satisfaction and give me exquisite, lacy-patterned strength in my spirit.

Yes, it has been a long day, and I am not at my best, but I'm like someone limping away from a fight that she won by just a hair. I may even be playing dead just so they don't try to find me. I'm going toward a land that I have defended but not even lived in yet. I am banged up and I can't see well and I'm stumbling too fast for someone so tired, but I am the one to live in the land now and I am the one to write the creed and when I wake up tomorrow, I will know that today was the day that I knew and felt all of the hard things, and that I was visited by many astounding pains but that I also realized the truth: It is finally the time for a creed, and this will change everything.

The Code of Hammurabi

I am sitting in the room in my house where I've put the television in a big wicker cabinet so that I don't ever have to see the television. I enjoy watching the TV, but also I think that it is an ugly object. I cringe when I see the TV loitering like a dumbass, incorrect in its placement next to my books and tender hanging plants and thoughtfully chosen textiles. But here I am, sitting in front of it. I am watching a documentary that anyone can find and watch. I have not dug deep into a subculture to find it. It was right here when I turned on the thing and clicked on the other thing.

And the world is certainly scary because suddenly *everything is computer* and computers and internet stuff, but there is still some good to extract from it, like this documentary I am watching.

I have Thai food that is so spicy that I start to sweat and breathe in and out like how ladies do Lamaze breathing while having a baby in a movie in the 1980s. I ordered it with the vague notion that it might be really nice to just blow my colon out once and for all. It might be nice to live life as a big empty whistling network of inner caves. But now I see that I am just bloating myself with salt and fusing my insides together with oils that I am not genetically inclined to process.

I think, If my ancient dog gets even a lick of this curry, his hair-fur will fall off of his body like when you blow on a dandelion. And then he will throw up a small trickle of yellow. And then he will die. And then I will have no-body at all including the many different men who have held this dog to whom I have said, *This is amazing. He really likes you!* When what I really mean is

You are holding my dog. I can't tell if you are nice or gross yet. We'll see.

This is what I think as my insides burn to bits, as my guts curl up into cracklins for a goblin to chomp in hell.

Every morning I call my best friend and we have

coffee on separate sides of the city and we talk about how Patriarchy is killing us. She told me that this documentary was one to watch, and so here I am, watching this documentary on my TV that I basically keep in a big giant basket. The narrator is a British woman who seems borderline horny to tell me what she is about to tell me, and her documentary series is called *The Ascent of Woman,* which actually makes me "emotionally horny" as well.

The woman is a smarty and she is very earnest. She also wears lipstick.

This is what the British woman tells me in her documentary TV show, or at least this is what I can summarize:

Patriarchy is not something that was inevitable. It is not what a God wants or ever wanted, even though that has been said by many men. It is also not what Nature intended (and now that must be clearer than ever, because look at what Patriarchy has done to our Planet Earth). Nature does not want to be tortured and raped and murdered. Nature does not want to be wholly exploited. Patriarchy is not ever going to be for Nature's own good. Nature belongs to Nature, first and foremost. Nature wants to give to us, but that does not mean we should take more than we need. Nature wants to engage, but not fully submit.

The British woman says: Patriarchy is not a human-biological inevitability. Patriarchy is not here because it "just makes sense" or is the product of a thoughtful rationale.

There was a time before Patriarchy.

We have a better origin story and it is not widely spoken about but it is the truth.

This lady on my TV tells me that Patriarchy was constructed and implemented, and explains that humans originally lived *as a community,* in a group, and everyone used the tools and everyone took care of each other's babies, and shared their foods and prayed to gods and goddesses that were equally powerful and holy.

As the communities got larger and created more people, these people were able to accomplish more, to store food and make better shelters from the wildness out there, to live longer and have more children. And they did this for a very long time. It was natural. And it became bigger and bigger and there was especially one good spot, between the Tigris and Euphrates rivers, and this was called the Fertile Crescent. It was called the "cradle of civilization" and you might have learned about it in the fourth grade and you might have become obsessed with it, like I did.

You might have overfocused on the cosmic significance of this one spot that sort of seems like it is the Earth's Vagina. And the civilization of people, in that spot between the two rivers, broke the banks and led the water out into the land. The people led the water far out and they created irrigation. They trained water to come farther and to new places. This allowed the people to have more crops. Then there was a surplus of crops.

I did learn about this, in fourth grade, from the best teacher I have ever had, Mrs. Damp, who never shamed me and was teeny tiny and had a necklace that said her name in hieroglyphics.

I would love to have a beer, and so I do get up and get one and my mind wanders into spots where these questions are shimmying: Would Teddy Roosevelt be a feminist? Would he like me or think I am a wimp? Were the Kennedys just really gross, like, with women? Yes, they were. It's not great, when you think about it, what they were like with all of the actresses. It's gross. Why are so many men so gross but still we say that they are heroes? And if we try to even talk about it with these men, they get incredibly upset and defensive and call us cruel or insecure, but really, you can't have it both ways.

You can't do the thing but then not want to ever discuss it. If you want to hide it, maybe it's not just because "it is private" but because you know, you really do know, that it is gross.

This is what I think about as I crack a Miller High Life and vaguely decide that I should not continue to have cyclical relationships with gross men, and that I will be sort of an "aunt to the world" and begin to collect sex toys made by other feminists.

Or maybe I will meet and fall in love with an actually good man, I think, as my stomach lurches with curry-fire and my nipples are randomly hard from the amount of spice in my body.

In the room with the TV, the dog is sniffing for curry, but it is only a memory. I have removed the bowls. The TV goes right back on because I press the buttons and I'm the boss, and here's my British gal, now wearing a head scarf while touring an archeological dig. Her mouth has a daytime lipstick on it and she wants me to know this:

Civilizations (Sumer, Mesopotamia, etc.) flourished in the Fertile Crescent between the Tigris and the Euphrates. Some people must have ended up with more than other people, because of the surplus of crops after they invented irrigation, and so then there was not only a class system but also greed, a new toothy, fast-breathing, slick-thinking, not-sorry greed.

151

This woman reminds me of this sequence of events that for some reason I have always been fascinated by ever since Mrs. Damp told us about it—that there was a surplus and the world changed.

Where there should have simply been an equal distribution of goods and general dedication toward community satisfaction and safety, instead greed came in and took ahold of a few key players. And these key players who were cold enough to look past questions of whether or not what they were doing was humane were Men.

"Men with penises and ballsacks," I think, while looking down to see that I have somehow splattered my pajamas with curry and have only noticed it right now.

Men did it. And they saw the Women having babies out of their bodies. And they saw the babies growing up into what could be a workforce, and they decided to take a crucial and revolting step, which was to *make Women and children into property,* and to condemn their own spirits and identities to be mostly defined by what happens to their property.

I start to understand that before the "greed event," lots of bad things had already occurred, killings and rapes and theft and abominations of all kinds, but these bad things were never harnessed into a system. And then, says this British woman, they were. I was made into

a system. Somebody did it. He is not a mystery person—
his name was Hammurabi and he was a real man and he
did it. He said that he did it. It wasn't an admission; it
was a declaration. He was proud.

My colon is now apparently filled with lava?

What this man created is this: the Code of Hammurabi. It was etched onto an obsidian phallus. It is
physically scratched into a big hard ancient dick. And to
be fair (although why must I, after all of this, be fair?!),
the Code of Hammurabi has many different laws etched
into its dark knob. Some are laws that are meant to keep
the peace, but they are all spoken in a deeply misogynist
voice, and so, in my opinion, they are unjust and they are
void.

The Code of Hammurabi is one of the first examples
of legalized patriarchy, and it instilled these violent and
demented ideals: A woman is the property of a man. A
woman does not deserve to have as much as a man and
she should not ever have as much as a man ever again.

It says that in order for the men to thrive, women must
be kept in line and controlled. It says, *This starts now.*
It says women are worth something great to us, and because of that we must say that they are less than us, and
we must never let them know what it is about them that
we are trying to take for ourselves. It says, *Women can't.*

They *must not*. It says, *Women are property*. Men decide what women can do with their bodies. Men own women. We are all separate and must stay divided. Women are beneath, less than, but also, watch out for them, really do watch out! But act like you are not "watching out" or scared—act like a good guy who is protecting the holy object.

It says, *Act like you are innocent*. It suggests, *Tell them they are crazy*.

It seems that I can't finish the second beer. Suddenly I am exhausted, angry, and near faint. I am thinking of ancient men and ancient stones and granaries and bird-gods.

After I walk the geriatric dog, who is my old friend, and after I wash my dear little face, I get into my bed, which could fit four of me. I lie in the bed and scratch my legs with my feet and feel morose and incredibly young. I get ready to sleep fitfully.

I think about the Tigris and Euphrates and what they whisper to each other now when they meet, constantly, at their problematic delta. "Holy fucking shit, man," says the Tigris. "This is *not* our fault," says the Euphrates, reading the other river's mind.

It seems to me, as I lie here with my dog, who may very well have been born in Mesopotamia because he is so very old, that once you make it permissible to look away, *that* is when you irrigate your spiritual landscape with something foul.

The Code of Hammurabi is the first evidence of legalized patriarchy. Does that send a shiver through your bones? Does that make you feel like we are currently ruled by fucking mummies who hate our mommies? Because that is what it is.

Does it not seem unnatural that the basis of the interactions between genders in our species is something that was created by a psycho who took too much from an already generous river, thousands of years ago? Does it make you sick to know that the same men benefiting from this code are also the duds who are adjusting their popped collars, fixing their necklaces, wearing a ton of deodorant, and confidently saying, *Okay, babe, but...to play the devil's advocate...like...think about hunter-gatherer stuff. Like, isn't it just the way that nature works?*

Nature does not work that way. Nature does not give a shit about low thinking like that. Nature invited us to be more than apes, more than cave people. Nature pushed us to change. Instinct is real but so are the facts that we lived communally and that human remains have been found buried with tools, both genders buried with tools, buried with babies from the other humans who dwelled next door. We lived in groups, we acted in a friendly way toward each other. We partied together. That is what we were inclined to do.

Me too, even though I currently live alone and do not want to really use tools and I don't know how to change a diaper and I'm afraid of that thing that happens when sometimes a baby poops and the poop goes all the way up their little back like a bad backwards shit-dickey.

The Code of Hammurabi's Penis was put in the Louvre, where Mona Lisa is about to fully smile and most likely totally crack up any day now. Because this code thrust Patriarchy into that ancient world, it influenced the creation of every other piece of art in that museum. Every piece of art that was created after the Code was somehow affected, and also all of our clothes and food and politics and religion and marketplace and how we have sex and who we do it with and how we talk to each other and what colors we think we are allowed to connect to and wear and use in our work and put on our signs and see in our minds.

I don't care if it is ancient or has some good points. I don't care anymore about tradition that represents many things but certainly the oppression of more than half of humanity.

Call me a vandal but I am lying in my bed and I say, *I think maybe we should throw it in the trash.* Can something that is important enough to be in a museum go right to the trash now?

Of course, I am just a woman lying in the dark, listening to my stomach squeal and counting the seconds before my midnight curry diarrhea extravaganza, but should we just throw this ancient statue of a choad into a French dumpster?

Or sure, sure. Okay. *The trash* doesn't feel exactly right, so, okay.

What about: Keep it in the museum but say *what it really is* and what it has done, and make the museum visitors scream *NOOOOOO* at it, so that people on other floors of the museum are drawn to the spot of the shouting. People from Indiana and India and Iran—on vacation in France—say, *What's that exhibit where you get to scream at something?*

They look at their museum maps but they can't find any information. So they just do what animals do and they follow the sound. They form a crowd around a glass case that holds a random old stone boner and they find themselves screaming *NOOOOOO* as well. It is refreshing and out of the ordinary to do this, and they like it because it feels good to make big noises as a group.

And the sound waves are so forceful that they wash away the etching of the old, evil laws.

And then when the etching is erased, let the sound waves of that universal NO bounce off that dusty dick-statue and into the bodies of the people screaming *NOOOOOO*. Let the sound waves wash the inside of the people too, washing out the misogyny, washing out the ingrained laws that cause all of us, any gender identity, to have anxiety and rage and sadness because of where we have been sent and kept. Blast away the deep ridges inside that create a feeling of unnameable dirtiness and shame.

Let it wash the obsidian phallus until it feels naked without its code and it just shrinks down, puffs into black dust. Then, place what is left into a little vial. Put that vial in a boring part of the museum. And the label on the vial should read, "These are the crumbs of the code that choked humans for thousands of years. This used to live in our minds and hearts. Now it is here and it is nothing but dust. If I were you, I would check out the *Mona Lisa,* which is surprisingly small for such a famous painting, but still thrilling. Take in her mystery! What *is* she thinking?"

Focus on this old painting of this woman who doesn't care about serving you, who keeps her story to herself because you are not her boss and she is smiling first and foremost for herself and she'll grin when she fucking feels like it.

I finish the documentary eventually. I learn about ancient female warriors and poets, and quite a bit of new information about foot binding in China, and about St. Hildegard of Bingen, who was a mystic and a genius and who also really turns me on, intellectually speaking.

But the Code of Hammurabi really sticks with me. When I encounter a proud misogynist or an unconscious one, or I see misogyny flare up in myself, I imagine this Code sitting in the museum, or sitting on a block, being created far back in the past, and I say to myself that this can all go another way.

I lie in my bed and I say, *There was a start and so there can be an end.*

Kinship

I sit at the table in the afternoon in the part of the day when the air is warm still from hanging in a day of sun. I have a clock in my kitchen and the kitchen is a different room from the dining room, because this house is from before World War II and even before World War I, when people were smaller and lived shorter lives and didn't know the term "great room" or "open concept."

I sit in a room that was built even before movies were made here in this city, which has been filled with movie people and people thinking about movies, with movie people's shredded dreams, shreds of dreams left to moan in pieces all over this palm-tree-dotted patch at the edge of a whole country. I sit where people came like babies and zombies, drawn to an art form that is incredibly dangerous and decadent and astounding and represents stories in motion, represents life in a way that we find irresistible, and also is responsible for a massive amount of darkness and abuse.

I sit in a chair in an old house at a table that is from Denmark and from someone else's house in the 1960s on another part of the planet in a time that has rolled away behind us. I sit in the chair, which is probably as old as my friend's young baby, who is crawling so fast and is startlingly robust and most likely currently holding a banana too hard and making it into a lint-y, silly pudding in his little baby hand.

I sit here in the afternoon, which seems to be holding its breath, and I hear the day birds and their noises like necklaces shifting, like glass being tinkled, but I also hear the motors of the wings of the night bugs starting to rev up because they feel the sun glancing over its shoulder to leave. I sit here and I turn around to face the air coming through the window, and the air is so warm that I take it as a sign that it is all right to be alive as I am, just as I am, and to keep trying.

I have recently clung to my very foundations and lasted many upsets, and I have had a muddled mind, even. But I see the light on the leaves and how it makes them seem filled up with green, not just flat with green on the flat. I see how they appear to be filled with air and how light and air are separate but make holy beauty out of nature that is already so sacred. I see it. I know it. That nature makes art and I am a creation and I make things. This is an expansive fact that I could never measure, and it calms me. The elemental companionship of light and air make it so beautiful on those leaves that when I turn in my chair to really look, the leaves are just there existing, and I feel my heart break down even more and I say, *Good, let it fall away, and look, look, everything is always remaking itself and so are you. Everything is art and nature and so are you.*

And I see the leaves turn a bit in the air, and the breeze coming in feels like the whole world is a pet that is breathing on me, and I think, *Well, I am so sensitive and I am very fragile but so is everything else, and living with a dangerous amount of sensitivity is sort of what I have to do sometimes, and it is so very much better than living with no gusto at all. And I'd rather live with a tender heart, because that is the key to feeling the beat of all of the other hearts.*

And I do know that I have been drawn here, hooked through my spirit just like some woman was drawn here in 1937, 1959, 1976, looking for a break in this place, to be a part of the art of moving images, looking for someone to say, *We should all watch you.* Wanting to be watched but also wanting to be *watched,* like by a guardian, like that the whole world wants to watch you to make sure you are safe. If the whole world knows who you are then it is harder to get lost out there, although time and Hollywood have proven that many of the people get lost inside of themselves because of an unbalanced reaction to exposure outside, in the world of others.

This is all romantic and degrading and interesting at the same time—nothing cancels another thing out.

It is gross and great.

I let myself stop holding everything so tightly, I let it all fall away and I feel the warmth of the sunbeams at this time of day and I feel deep pride and spiritual fortification in the fact, not even the idea, but the fact that the light shines on me just as it does on the leaves and that even though I came here to try to do the art that I want and I want to be seen and held safe by my world, truly, in my primary wish for experience, I am asking for nothing more than a kinship with the atmosphere.

A Fact

When gentlemen go to the doctor they need to take off their pants and show it all and turn around and cough to prove to the doctor that the balls are not dead in their bag.

(Having a body is bizarre.)

Geranium

A mistake has been made about wildness.

I was in another country. I was in a small town on a northern sea. All around me were sheep with big bells. They walked silently through the night, I could hear them passing, and they were not bleating and they were not straining against the dark. I could hear only their bells but I could imagine their bodies and their forward linear movements in the dark. I could smell their muddy wools.

Where I was, there was also a rose garden. There was a castle there built in the 1600s for a woman named Karen. How does that feel? *Hey, Karen. It's, like, 1617. I built you a castle with rose gardens. Inside the castle I couldn't pay for marble so I painted the wood to look like marble. Karen? It was the best I could do for the person who I believe is the best.*

You're the best, Karen. I made you a castle.

The windowsills in the castle were deep and made of stone.

In my own life in another country and hundreds of years later, what had happened was this:

I was born at the time of year when small heroes bravely stick their neck-stems out for all of us, bet every molecule of blind faith on nature's natural rhythms, and win for all of us, making us clap.

So, that happened first. Then I started to learn and I ate a lot of salty things and became obsessed with things like seashells and breasts and the word *refreshment* as a food and drink option that is supposed to make you feel a feeling, and I started to fall in love all over the place. I also rode bikes, failed at group sports, but succeeded in a love of water and swimming. I was scared of dogs and then obsessed with them.

I got in trouble for being wild.

I got in trouble for my feelings at school and camp and then always. I got in trouble for not paying attention to things that seemed boring to me but now are gorgeous to me, like clocks and compasses and calendars.

I had, always, a wild call that I wanted to ring out to the whole world. I knew it always.

I wanted to be an actress. I often felt like a bird in a house and I felt that people reacted to me that way so I started to try to find ways to do my wild work in inside spaces. I started to find spaces where I could bring wildness inside. I started to find a way to still be myself but be with the group.

I tried the start of a life with someone and it didn't exactly take, but it didn't exactly flee, and I had to let it go and be out there and hope some part of it would wander back to me like an animal that went out young and had to live in the wilderness and came back, and whenever it is that it would come back, this life, this love, I had to stare into its face and say, *Is it you?* And then we would be friends, at peace with the idea of being two creatures who started together but needed different environments.

But that is in the future and I am talking about the past.

Then I was all alone. I bought a house that was built

roughly three hundred years after Karen's castle was built. The house was empty and waiting for me when I eventually ended up in Norway, looking at roses and the cold seas and laughing about how actually old the name Karen is.

I was in another country. In conversation I made a wish, I said it out loud to a group of new friends. I said that I wished that red geraniums could be a houseplant. I said that I knew that they were for outside. But couldn't they be for inside if I tried to truly understand them? We all sort of said that they probably could? But nobody knew.

The geranium is a hardy little mother. You can hardly kill it. It takes a lot to kill one.

I had never seen a geranium in a house as a serious thing that was really happening, on purpose.

We were invited to have dinner that night in Karen's castle.

In every window of the castle, in every single window, on every single deep stone windowsill, was a red geranium. My heart stopped, or maybe it jump-started. I saw those geraniums and I felt my wild call ring right out, into *up there*.

I saw them and I was nothing but double doors to spirit, to everything, blasted open, tilted up. I thought,

"Why would you not believe in this thing? Why would you not believe in such a small thing like putting this hardy red plant in your house?" I had called for what I wanted, based on who I was. And Karen's castle had given me a big blazing sign that said, *Yes ma'am.*

At camp I used to pick off the red flowers from the geranium and sneak into the bathroom and rub the petals on my lips, making lipstick, tasting the plant. Even as a little girl who got in lots of trouble, I picked this plant out and said, *I like to use this for my own beauty.*

I am a wild thing but I wanted a home. I am wild and I want to be that and to belong to the greater group and have everyone know that my wildness is nothing but a bit of my colors and has nothing to do with whether or not I can be trusted. A geranium is a wild thing. It is so wild you can hardly kill it. But it does not take over your house if you put it inside.

A geranium in every single window of a castle is a wink to me, even if it is just a plant to you, maybe even a plant in the wrong place. Sitting in a kitchen in Norway, over breakfast, my heart broke at the idea of someone thinking that the plant was in the wrong place. I talked about that heartbreak. I felt my heart clutch itself. It was breakfast and I didn't want to cry. There was a handsome stranger sitting across from me.

But I am wild, and a tear fell right when I tried to open my mouth. My body will always show what my real inner situation is. My body will never let me lie. I was almost gasping. I realized I am wild but I do not want to be sent to the wilderness and I looked across at my friend and at the handsome stranger and I made up my religion right in front of their faces and I said the first line of my own holy book:

I believe that wildness belongs in people.

I believe that wildness belongs in the home. I believe this and so I belong in myself and in my home. My gods are inside of me first and foremost, and the mother of all of them is the wild one.

There has been a misunderstanding about wildness. Bring it in, bring it in, bring wildness in, and care for it.

Place a shell in your shower. Get a whole plant in there. Put a geranium in your kitchen. Stand in your space and howl out. Bring it in or go out and see it. Wildness is the mother, the first thing, not a lurking predator. Wildness is holy.

I am a geranium that is hardy and wild, but I want to sleep in a neat little pot. I belong in a castle that was built with the determination and ingenuity of a person who was deeply in love.

I feel the warmth vibrating through the centuries and that's why it is hard to kill me even with a frost. I feel the warmth from the heart of a woman named Karen, three hundred years ago, who got everything she wanted, who brought these plants inside maybe, who brought wildness into the place her love built just for her.

He put her name over the doorway.

A Tender Thief

One time, my dog sneaked six licks of coffee from my mug. I caught him on the sixth and I'm certain that he would have gone all the way. But I did catch him on the sixth. After he'd had his coffee he went and he stretched out on the armchair and spent a long time by the window, and I thought, "At least he knows how to have coffee properly, even though he is a thief."

Night Treats for Her

Most nights, I stand in the middle of the kitchen in the middle of the night, completely asleep. I stand there naked like Persephone wandering between worlds. I am holding a spoon in the air, gripping a small jam jar and digging through jelly to find berries, spooning dark red preserves into my little mouth. I drink half glasses of cold milk and stick my dreaming hands in the raisin jar. I do leave a trail. I eat upwards of seven cookies. I will throw the tinfoil off of the cake and drop the crinkled silver sheet onto the floor and assault the cake itself, carving into it with a spoon that is slick and sticky with jam. When I am in the supermarket, I slow down cautiously in the jam aisle. I don't even eat toast or muffins, which is what jam is really for. I could stop buying the jam, but then what would happen? I don't know what to do about what I seem to need, how much sweetness, how many treats. I cannot rest without waking as my deepest self, the woman who is wailing for what is not provided as a normal morsel during the day. My nighttime menu knows its loyal customer: I drool for scoops of dripping colors. I want to bite into the things that they say are too sweet to have just on their own. The heart part of me walks the night, sweet and scary, consuming the things that are delicious yet apparently too concentrated to be encountered alone, as themselves. But they match me. I need to prove to myself that there is an appetite for sweet things that are lonely in the night. In the bright light of the day, I select the jar of jam. "It's for *her*," I say to myself as I shiver with anticipation. I imagine the moon rising, the loss of control against the deeper desires, a naked still dreaming darling darting through the rooms, an appetite finally met, the top twisting off the jar that is waiting in the dark.

The Root: A Made-Up Myth

I want to be a part of a system of power that does not disgust me. I have to give myself many pep talks. I am not sure of what to do most of the time, but I do not want to do what I was doing before. I need a new story, please. I suppose I have to give it to myself.

Before we all got here, there was a garden and the garden was good. I know that this is also the beginning of the Bible. The Bible is not the only book that is authorized to talk about good gardens. There are magazines about good gardens. There are TV shows. This is just another garden story.

The garden was growing and there were people in there and they were tending to the growth. It was living and they were living, and they were full of blood and bones and air and germs too, and it was fine. A cruel deity spied on everyone from a shitty patch of the sky, where it was more mud-colored rather than that celestial blue-black that helps our stars to stand out. He was a "he" and he saw all of the people as an "us" and so he was bitter and wrathful when he realized his loneliness. And he saw the mighty garden. He saw how fertile the soil was and how varied the garden-culture was, and he just twisted even tighter in his knobbed and dry identity.

He sent down a bad pod to shove itself and burrow in the garden. And while one man was harvesting more than he needed one day, he held the extra in his hands and he turned his eyes to the side toward something that whispered to him. It was the imposter pod. It had become a plant.

Think of it like this: The story is not that a woman named Eve ate an apple, but that a man bent down, his hands filled with the weight of having more than his share.

This made-up ancient man who I am putting in this useful story did not walk toward the community but instead he opened his mouth and the pod-plant slithered right in. A live vine went right into this human fellow. The vine sprouted greed and loneliness and panic in the man. The vine said, "You should have it all. *It* should all be you. Everyone else is trying to make you less of you and you need to stop them."

The first man with the root of the alien vine in his body went out and opened his mouth again in front of others and the vine shot right into every single person that he spoke to and they all took the vine and the lie into themselves. The root got stronger and stronger. It became a system of grabby tendrils that made a net and everyone was in it. It controlled how they talked and walked and made love and made art. It was in the way they had their babies—and because after a while they didn't even know that it was there, it was in the babies. And thousands and thousands of years later it was every-where, in everything.

I open my mouth and reach an invisible hand down into the deepest part of me. I get into myself even though it is scary. If I deny that the root is in me, I will never change. I know that nobody is immaculate and so I don't shame myself anymore—I just try to weed myself so that I don't wither and weep. I reach down and start to pull the root.

I am pulling and it tortures me, make no mistake. When I yank the vine a bit, when I disturb the root in its little grave inside of me, it shows me all of the memories of all the times that I honored the pod like a drooling fool. Holy moly, this shitty vine grips tight to my soft pink brains and infuses my thinking. It says that I am a hypocrite and it says it in the voice of authority figures, ex-lovers, even my own mother. But I am allowed to rehabilitate and move forward, so I give myself reasonable counsel: "This is nothing but spooky stuff from a freaked-out root. This is what happens in an exorcism, babe. The bad thing wears the faces and forms of your failures and family and it says *you are hurting me.*" I keep an eye on my stamina and I pull slowly and consistently.

I watch the pod whisper to men that if they really pull it out, it will pull off their penises. I am just one woman pulling an ancient cultural root out of her spirit, and I am not a doctor or a shaman, but I can say, just as a citizen and an ally, that nothing will happen to your penis if you stop being a misogynist. It will still be the same penis. Maybe if you stop listening to the insidious whisper of a centuries-old pod, you will have less stress about your penis, though? Just a theory but I'd actually bet money on it.

It is strenuous and isolating to do this work within

myself. I pull and the root tells me that I look ugly while I am pulling, and that nobody will want to have sex with me anymore. That is scary because I want to be nice-looking and have romances, but my job is to listen and hear how these are cruel threats and outright lies. My job is to pull. Every time one more inch is pulled out from inside of me, I feel relief. I start to look different. I look more specifically like myself. I look less like someone who hopes that a pod will accept her, and more like a flower who busted up out of the soil, in the middle of the night, fed by equal portions of sunlight and moonbeams. It actually feels more sexual than ever.

Eventually I reach so deep that I rip out the root. I dangle it in front of my face. It is a shrunken, sad root, quite small compared to my heart, dull in color and unable to pump life. I take one last good look at that poison pod and I just go ahead and *fling it*. I fling that pod back into that gloomy section of outer space that is for bad gods with sickly and sour spirits. I wipe my mouth off and I say out loud, *This stupid old root was nothing but a cosmic clog.*

I need a helpful myth to show me what came before. I need a new made-up story to deliver me into the real life that I would like to live.

Fur

I dreamed I lifted up my little breasts and lining their undersides was a soft white- and toffee-colored fur, not hair, and I thought: "Oh man, how am I going to deal with this?" and then I was sad that I couldn't keep it.

It was my own fur, of course, but I knew that I would have to get rid of it.

My fur was so soft and clean. I felt it with my hands and it was as if I touched a dearness for and in myself as well as a sorrow that I had forgotten. And in the dream, I realized that women have simply never been told that they have soft white- and toffee-colored fur beneath their breasts.

Somehow my fur had crept in quietly and achieved its regrowth. It didn't even notify me, maybe because it thought that I would put a stop to it. It was benevolent, the way it slipped in and went to work in and on me so that I could be whole again after feeling emotionally shorn and corralled.

In the dream, I put my fingertips into my fur and I stroked it against the grain of the growth and I let it spike up and turn down onto its pattern again. It knew where to go back onto itself on me and I felt a relief when I realized, *I have been trying to destroy myself and I don't want to anymore.*

In the dream, I wanted so badly to have and keep my fur. I wanted so badly to not even know about the possibility that I could get rid of it.

When I am in my morning, I brush my teeth with no shirt on and look at my torso and touch that area on myself where the fur was in the dream, and I ask out loud, *Who will let me be the real animal of myself?* I am asking it out loud into the air but of course the only person that I see is me in the mirror and so I become the first one to say yes to my bare self, which is proper and right.

All day long and in my life after I have this dream, I

pet myself in the space that lives under my breasts and down to my waist and I feel calmed when I think of my fur. I sometimes imagine a man petting my fur. I will know him as the man who is allowed to be here because he is the one who will be at ease with my fur and pet me when I am nervous and not be mad at either of the following: that I have not removed my fur and that I live here in this non-dream world where it does feel that often people hunt me for my hide and I am nervous a lot.

Tart

There was a tart little taste in my mouth when I remembered the appointment at your office. Your office, which is a white rectangular room with pleasing, wide square windows of clear light. Your office, which is a space for plants that are green hang-down pals and indoor tree-things. And of course I am also a plant and so I like to be in there too, drinking small glasses of water, sitting around, taking in sun, absorbing our conversations.

But when I thought about the appointment in your office, I was not a plant but I was suddenly a cross little woman. There you would be, at the appointment in that space in the future, where you would be yourself and I could be anyone because it is the future, but there you also were back in time, in the past, when it was dark and we were angry, and the whole thing made me uncomfortable here in the present and I felt fussy.

Luckily there is a supermarket in the present, and supermarkets please me. Luckily, I am of sound enough mind, even in my puckering tartness, to drive a car to the supermarket, buy egg-yolk-colored daffodils, and cream for my coffee and get myself into a livelier tempo in general.

I pushed the cart. I said things to myself like, "Stop looking for things to be sad about, that's not what it actually is anymore," and of course I was right, that's not exactly it. There is nothing sad anymore, there are only tiny and tart truths. I saw that I was wise to instruct myself in this way. So I said, "And furthermore, start looking for eggs." I did. I found myself some eggs, and tender butter-leaf lettuce and a prissy endive and some jokey Kirby cucumbers and some standard butter and a new giant olive oil because I was anticipating filling my mouth with salty, lemony, glistening leaves.

The sourness about the appointment got in line with the rest of my feelings. It made itself into a goldenrod color in my chest. "Oh, I see," I said. It wanted to be beautiful, this sourness. It was ready to be a part of something useful. Oh, I do see.

I got what I needed in that moment and I went home to do more of what was required.

I picked two Meyer lemons off the tree outside of my house where I live alone and where you do not live with me. There are other ways to say that but since I was still a bit sour I had to frame it up like that, make a statement in black-and-white. But it can never hold, that black-and-white way. I never want it like that. I'm just too much of a color wheel now to limit myself to statements like that, and I know it, so I buck up and I say, "Well, what can you do? What will you do now with all of this tartness and all of this yellow?"

I would never be this whirling wheel of colors if we had not changed the shape of who we are together. I knew that, but still, there was a bit of bitterness left in the rotation.

In the night, while I ran the bath and waited for it to fill up as a warm place for me, I chopped up the lemons, orange-yellow rinds and all, all color, all juice, all flavor, all pucker and pleasure. I held that whole fruit and I said, "I will use the whole of it because nothing is unprocessable, and I will not discard any parts, because there is a wholeness here if I can be resourceful and think about things differently," and then I did that, and I baked a tidy little lemon tart. I sweetened it. While it was becoming a treat in my oven, I took my body to the bath and I did my best to wash any grit away from myself.

I brought the tart to your office and we sat there and we each ate one long yellow triangle piece. You stood up and took my picture while I sat back like a good little plant holding a piece of a lemon tart on my tender green leaf-hand. I thought maybe the tart was too tart-tasting. But I had been right about the amount of sweetness to add so that we could sit there and have it and have a conversation and not have our mouths screwed shut from any sourness.

One can put sweetness into something, on purpose. I can never take away the color of the feeling. Yellow is yellow so what are you going to do with it? It was in me and it was almost acidic and corrosive and I held it long enough inside of myself so that it went from a burning canker to a glowing color and the color was yellow and so I followed the color from one of its forms to the next. I ended up with a treat. I shared it. It was not easy, but it was certainly not hard.

Then again, it was certainly its own zone, it was certainly disorienting, to do this process of tart to sweet, because when I came home I felt bananas. And just to see if I was onto something, I put on some music and I put on the oven and I threw some bananas into a batter.

I'm sure you can't bake it all away, but you can transform the reality while still accepting the essential elements that make it what it is. You can make good smells in the place where you live, smells that are better than sitting around with stress breath and cigarette smoke. Who knows? Who knows how to do anything, but it's not nothing that I know all my feelings and I have trust in their changeable nature and I am an expert at making treats out of tribulations.

It's in the oven. The dog is asleep next to a large strawberry pillow that he likes as a friend. I will have the bread soon enough. I wonder what you will do with the picture you took of me. I wonder what you will do with the rest of the tart. I guess the trick of the treat is that I left it there for you because I had too much of the troublesome ingredient with me for so long and I needed to make it into something else and give it away. It is too much for one person, isn't it? And if you eat it, maybe you will know how full of it I felt, but also how much sweetness I have been holding for you, inside of myself, in so many colors and forms.

Clothes Flying On/Day Flying Open

Hello, I am a woman and I have been awake for at least two hours, during which I have spoken on the telephone, fixed breakfast for the old dog, made strong coffee and put it in the white and blue coffee cup that is so delicate and short that it is really a teacup but is indeed for my coffee. I took many sips.

Hello, I have been up for a while and I stood in my nightgown on the front porch and sniffed the air like taking in wafers of just-born light and I haven't even thought of brushing my teeth but I have actively and absentmindedly fussed over my new triangle haircut. I left my coffee on top of a china cabinet, next to a plant, and I will not see it again until I move it this afternoon and that has nothing to do with whether or not I am tidy. I am certainly tidy and that tidiness comes from deep inside of me because I know where everything is always, starting from inside of myself. Very tidy.

Hello, I changed from the white cotton nightgown with light blue embroidery on the collarbone into a very smart outfit for living in the day: a cream-colored skirt, with a grid of white, and pleats all the way around, an accordion of cotton. The pleated skirt is the color of tea with lots of cream. Traditionally speaking, it is the color of tea with *too much* cream and sugar in it. The skirt is the tone of a slightly warm dessert-drink hiding in a cup, a secret gentle creamy treat for me while everyone else drinks a darker, more serious, scalding thing.

Nobody knows how extra sweet it is in *my* cup. I hide my delights in plain sight—I turn the normal thing into a much tastier option.

But do you know this: The outfit went right *onto* me. The outfit *flew onto me.* I put my hands in the air and I stood there and it flew on. I stood with my hands over my head like a young bride in her new country and I felt the air hit the fine soft skin that stretches down the inside of my arm and into my warm armpit and down my rib cage, where there is the circle of my little breast just waking up. And I felt, *I must get on with it! I must admit to my lust for knocking this morning into a full-on day!*

Hello, I live in a constant state of growth and regeneration without being obsessed with the threat of decay.

Well, what? It's my business how the heck I get dressed and how I remember it.

Something pushes me right out of the bedroom before I can turn around and reconsider almost everything about myself because that's what I do: I tear everything down sometimes in a fit of rip-roaring instinct, because I'm a terrifying, wild little thing. And sometimes I enact destruction just to reenact my faith that things can be built up again. But I'm trying to stop the first part of that and just have the faith. And I went downstairs and I thought, *Okay, here I go!*

* * *

Hello, I sit at my desk in these clothes, in this body, and the sweater slips down my shoulder and I turn my head right away and give myself between nine and thirteen kisses on my bare skin, and my eyes flick up from these kisses and look out the window, and outside the window there is a squirrel drinking in my fountain, underneath a grapefruit tree.

I think about how we are both having our mornings and that they are equal. I *do* feel it all and *then some.* I have just been kissing my own skin but now I feel the wet water in the squirrel's mouth. I feel the swollen grapefruit bear its heaviness, its tear-shaped pods of sweetness and tartness in one pink liquid, capsules surrounded by membrane, covered in a thick pinky orange rind. I put myself in everything that I see and I want it to put itself in me and watch that web of interaction spin out between us.

I am in contact with something and I accept something these days: I accept that somewhere there is the fastest animal and somewhere there is the brightest coral and all around are the energy streaks of lives of people who are now dead and somewhere is the most ripped up canyon and I can sense its depth and my very own heart jerks and shifts with all the waves going berserk in the ocean.

The magnolia blooms are so beautiful, the flowers are like fish in a tree. Sometimes do you ever get jealous of the plants, that they only have to grow and not know about it, and they don't take anything personally?

What can I do? I can only breathe in deeply. I can only bellow in a church that is deep inside of myself. I can only blast a shell-shaped horn that would shake down the oldest buildings. I can only leap for joy in my sacred inner caves and ring out the message: I am alive. I woke up again. I might as well be sprouting leaves, I might as well be covered in little clams.

Look at me. Yes, I am a woman who woke up and got dressed and sat down here. But look again, look from the seat inside of myself that I let you sit in for just a few moments: I am a woman in dessert tones at the start of a bleating little day. Mouth full of clover. Oh, holy shit, I am a big fat fruit on a tree, dangling in the air just so, living in a state of fullness and exhilaration. I am connected to eternity and I am part of everything and although I am with all of it, I am still different from anything and everything.

I am an example of a specific way of spending time and feeling existence in this world.

I Died: Bronze Tree

I know that I can't change it: I died.

I died as a very old woman.

I died after living more of my life with you than I lived with just myself.

I did die, and everyone wants to talk about that because it is the final thing, it is the only real completeness I guess, but completeness was never a prize, in my eyes. Connection always was, deepening, tending, asking, cycling through, all of the things that we did together before we died our deaths.

I died but it was so small compared to how I had lived so much and for so long with you, alive. One death was so small compared to all the things that we did in our life, things that we did all the way through, right to our ends.

I died seven years after you did—you went before, because that is the statistic that I know. I died knowing that that was the statistic, but still unsteady, wobbling on the unbelievable truth that you had left me. And you'd gone just when I was really about to become someone that needed a hand on me, not just to go down a stair but also to be on my soft old skin, to calm the hum of my bones that vibrated too roughly for such an elderly frame, because you know me, I just had so much energy that it was both a power and a liability.

I died but my blood was still fresh and fast, my heart was an up-close light, but my mind had wandered away by the time I died. My mind was lightly stepping in concentric circles, farther and farther into the navy blue air-sea behind me, where I moved in my own rhythms, whirling my long-ago past with my house's hallways now, mixing up rooms, putting odd things in my purse, insisting that someone dead had called on the telephone, insisting that there were "bugs with long feet and long tails" that came at sundown or that you who were already dead needed me to do something for you like mail a postcard to a teacher. I frightened people because I was in fact touching the frayed space between dimensions, talking to you from my side, which is not allowed. I would travel long distances in my mind, and it would make my face go blank. That was the compromise for living in the inner world, that my face in the outer world sort of paused.

I died and I was a spirit-rebel at the end, sneaking through the curtains in the worlds of spirits. You would have been proud. You always hated authority. You were always parking in front of the hydrant and then being royally PO'd when you'd have a ticket on the car or no car at all anymore. You always thought that breaking the rule was not just an act of defiance but of instruction, saying, "This rule is not life-affirming and so I will show you that it is just fine to live life without the rule."

But it never worked.

I died and before that, in the last dimly lit years, when I could have sworn that the house would fill with a thick sea-fog, when I saw a blue whale float by my doorway as I lay in bed, it was odd because you were not there but I was having an experience with you, about you.

There was no other time in my life when I looked for you and thought you were there, thought you must be upstairs or about to walk through the door, but you really just weren't there anymore. There was no other time when I'd shopped for groceries and bought grape jelly, which only you like, and brought it home just to realize the horror of what I'd done, buying purple jelly for a person who is not there.

I died and my sneaking and confused speaking and many demands after my journeys in my mind were not a surprise to our son and he never cut me off or called me crazy. He made me write it down. He took pictures of me. And he was glad to have them.

I died and our son sat in the living room of our house by himself and thought of a woman that he was not bold enough to love as you had loved me and I had loved you, and sitting there in a T-shirt and looking so much like you, he resolved to go out there and try to get her, to celebrate us by having his own love.

I died and I'd loved having a son with you. I had loved making both of you the same sandwich, I had loved saying to you through hidden laughs, "Go in there and tell him that he really needs to *practice* that cello, not just noodle around on it," and you'd pawed at me and I'd loved it and then you said, "*You* go in," and then I'd really lost my patience with both of you, which I also secretly liked, being cross about a cello, and by the time our son was bathed that night and you'd read to him and I'd listened to the story from our own room across the hall, I couldn't wait for you to come lie next to me in our soft clean bed.

I didn't let you read your book that night. We never had air-conditioning. I would get up and check on the fan in our son's room. I would get up just to smell you and give you kisses on your back in the shape of what I could remember of Orion. I could remember mostly just the belt, which is dear but not very impressive. Over and over again on your back every night, the belt. One, two, three cosmic smooches from me to you until you died and then I died, but sometimes in the time before I died and after you died I kissed three stars into the air of where your body used to be in the bed, thinking thoughts like, "If I can't have him then I will bring the sky down into the bed, one kiss at a time, and then it will be like I am in the cosmos with him." It was a fun activity that helped me fall asleep.

Sometimes, when my brain really started to ferment in its own syrup, when the inside of my mind would sprout powerful nightshades and blooms from a vital dementia, I would be sitting in a room full of people at a party, people talking about movies and new purchases and people having various relationships, and my face would arrange itself as if I were listening but really I was staring into a long black cone that would form in front of me when I was sitting still. I tried often to move around and do busywork but I was old and I was tired and I ended up sitting down a lot and then that's when the cone would come. The cone was a slowly turning tornado made out of something smooth and dark, and instead of coming down from the sky to lift up a car or just eat up a town, it stretched perpendicular to the horizon, with its base where the ocean turned into a line, and its very tip flicked out like a tongue and spun and spun and spun. The dark conical vacuum circled my face and sucked and sucked and whispered, "Let it out, let me take your sorrow to the darkest distance, let me take it off your hands," and it didn't seem friendly but I never knew how hard it would be to live with the loss of you, and I wanted to let go of the pain even though it was the last thing that felt alive from you, and so I, surrounded by people just doing their party-talk, let the cone take pain from me. "Tell me," it coaxed.

I spoke in my mind but also into the cone, "I miss being a wife. I miss saying *my husband*. I am tired of being in a constant state of recovery. I don't know how to be alone. I feel weak and fragile and crazy and deeply ugly. I don't know what to do now. I don't know what to do."

And the cone had its fill and finally collapsed into a long flat triangle and flew away like one wing of something, like a sail with no ship. I couldn't tell if the cone was a friend or an enemy and my guess is that it was neither but it did cause great trepidation in me, like when people have tigers as pets and they love them so much and then the tiger just randomly kills their partner and they are heartbroken but not really angry at the tiger, but also they must kill the tiger?

It's confusing. I was often confused. The cone left. The party was still there. Someone had dipped a cracker into something. They put the cracker on a small square napkin and put the napkin in the palm of my small old hand and said, "Try this." I looked bewildered. Someone said, "You like this, Mom. You've had it before." I thought, "I have never had this before. This is the only time this has ever happened to me. The rest of the time I was with my husband and I was myself." That's sort of how things started to go before I died.

I died and our son sat in the living room that I had kept nicely until the last devastating moments that were devastating and also frightening, not because of illness but because I lost the will to be tidy and admitted to being tired in a way that was different than the fatigue I dramatically complained about for my entire life.

Before, when I would complain of being tired it was always a subliminal plea to be treated nicely, to be loved, to have you all know how hard I've worked for you and that I wanted to be admired and thanked. My mother did that. You always hated that I did it. I admitted to starting to die when I stopped caring for my rooms, stopped doing that thing where I brought branches and leaves and flowers in to make the house alive. It was a statement that something was over. I made it to our son silently, through stopping my patterns. I made it to you in my voice inside of me, telling you, "See you soon, I think."

I died and our dog was still alive, and we'd had at least four dogs. I died and the dog was beside himself and he slept right next to me and would not leave the room and followed them out when they took me away. I died and right before I died I remembered having a snack with you in our creaky old bedroom late in the evening on our wedding night. I remembered feeling shy as the photographer took our picture in the fields beside the party earlier that night. We got married in our own fields. Near our own old house. I remember being afraid of getting a tick. I died and while I was leaving it all and my eyes couldn't even open I still remembered wearing a white bra the next morning as a new bride while I stood behind you at the sink, brushing my teeth as your new young wife. I died and I was old.

I died after living with you and never not living with you once I started. I died and behind me there were vacations with you, and before each vacation there was a conversation between us in which I begged you to take a vacation, was bitter toward you for seemingly wanting to work by yourself in a room more than you wanted to take a vacation to the ocean with me. But then we would go and you would always love it and you would always love me and when I died this was the story I knew. There was never another story when I died. There was never a time when we went away from each other and kept living somewhere else. I died and there were times when I had been furious at you, when I had leveled sheets of insults at you, prodded at your identity, been bored, felt abandoned, been mad about your unwashed socks and your problems with authority but I lived through it all and I dug deep, I didn't give up, and because I held on, I lived through countless pleasures and beauties with you and your brilliant mind, and we did as much as we could and then you died and then soon after that, I died too.

I died and I never had to know what it was like to live without you except for that very last part, which was heart-killing but natural. I died and I never knew what it was like to not be invited to your birthday party, to have to give you a present a week before or after the actual birthday. I died and I had always given you the present right on time. I'd woken up with you in the new morning of every new year of life that you tried out and carried out. I died having only lost you at the very end, not before.

I died and I died in a town by the sea. I died and you had already died in the bedroom upstairs, and when you died, the spark of your life flew into me when I watched your breath stop, and the spark did its last energy frizz inside of me and I didn't tell anyone but half of the lights of myself went off as well. Almost every door in me closed too. Most of the space, where you used to tread, to rest, to read, to sleep, most of that space closed up for good. I became a house with only the porch light on.

Did you know that when you left me I kept the house of myself dark, that I could not be brave enough to put on a light in case I caught a glimpse of myself, and that I left the windows open and had chills and night animals came in and screeched at me and I didn't call out for help because you weren't there? Did you know that when you left my life and I was still there alive, I saw everything through a screen of your atoms?

I died and I died in the bed that you died in too, honey. I was clean and the last thing I ate was some chicken broth (two sips) and one performative bite of a toast with strawberry jam on it (for our son, so that he could be less scared), even though it burned the inside of my little old mouth. The color of the red burned it, the jam color? Or the sugar burned it? I died and everything about me was a pale blue, which is nice because the colors of your death were tones of cream and white and so we looked great together.

I died looking out at the grave you had someone make for us. Years before, when we were in our thirties, you'd said that you wanted to have lots of young friends when we were elderly so that we could really be a part of life and know what was happening, and you said that you wanted our grave to be a life-sized bronze sculpture of a tree. I loved you so much when you said it. And before I died and before you died you said a whole parade of other beauties like those little hopes that you described.

We had crab apple trees on our grass around our house, by the drop-off cliff that went straight down to a small beach and then the Atlantic. One night in a booth in a local bar we were holding our old hands under the table and we were looking across to the faces of our young friends that you had wished for. We laughed because we were not dark-minded people but we told them, "This is odd but it really is serious." We told them, "We feel shy to say it." We told them, "We are clearly old and it's a cumbersome topic but we'd like you to make us some grave art."

And our young friends were still for a moment but then one said, "Well, you obviously have something in mind, right?" And then you switched to the tone I'd heard you take in our meetings or your lectures at a university. I realized that after a lifetime of meetings about making our art that we were having a meeting about our final art. I paid close attention to the smoothness of your voice and the way you laughed to let there be air and a break in the tension of making your proposal but you never wavered from what you wanted. I bathed in the pleasure of one last time of you creating something beautiful for us to be in together. I felt proud as you told them the concept for our eternal tree, our final bed.

The young woman friend looked at me watching you and she did cry. She did. And she hoped for what I had, and what we'd had, what we'd never lost, because that was not part of our story. I died remembering the end of that night, that we'd had pints of beer, just a bit too much, that our friends had driven us home along our old beach road, that they'd noticed our birch trees and rhododendrons and dogwoods, and that the car had been quiet, with open windows. That our young friends loved us, that we scared them a little, that we felt young inside ourselves after making such a wild request, and that we'd looked to each other in that back seat and could have died then from such radical happiness. We whispered, "Should we just collide and burst into atomic dust here in the back seat?"

We looked old but it was only a sort of drapery that life asked us to hold. We obliged but underneath we were still Orange Soda and *Seinfeld* TV Show and Ping-Pong. I whispered with my frail old smile, "Smash into me, asshole," and you said right back, "You wish."

I died after I lived my life with you, because that was the story, that was the story that happened and it was the only one and so it is what I knew when I died. Closed loop.

I died and I have to move on soon, but I will always be so glad for the life I had with you. The fact is that it is incredibly hard to RIP and I'm just not sure I can get it done. Because what will I be now? I know that we will have new life with new forms and that we won't be able to love each other like we did the last time. Maybe I am going to be a banana and you will be a car. It just won't work. I know that. And I'm not one to beg for the impossible, especially as a banana, but I can't seem

Jenny Slate

to stop reacting to the enormity of the final end of us, sweetheart. A death. A bunch of them.

I died. I died and what was left of you was already there with our bronze tree, an extension of you waiting for me at the airport with flowers. We'd put your remains under its big trunk, in a bronze cast of a small egg. I died and they put my ashes in another egg. My ashes were buried in the earth in a lovely object next to your ashes in a lovely object, and we were treasures at the end of our lives, at the root of our art.

Dog Paw

You are not quite awake yet, but the dreaming is done and so is most of your sleeping. You are waiting inside of yourself, waiting to wake up. You are still behind the curtain that separates awake and activity from sleeping and dreaming. You sense that you are waiting to wake up, but you also know that you are asleep. It feels tensionless, like watching a flag wave, like coming closer to a shore after a pleasure sail. You have a feeling like being happy for someone who has achieved an honor.

It is you.

You are happy for yourself that you have received the honor of a new day on which to ride. You realize that you love yourself easily in this gravity-free space between the worlds of waking and dreaming.

You are dear to yourself in the morning and it is the morning now. It is very private to have such a love for yourself. Closer, closer to the curtain. How funny, your face is right *right* against the curtain now. How funny to know what side of it you are on! You are asleep! How wonderful to pay attention.

On the other side of the curtain, a small, white elderly dog is moments ahead of you, and he decides, *he decides,* to come up to where *your* head is, to where your eyes are closed. He has observed you for over a decade, so he knows where your doors are.

He knows your hand is a door to your heart.

He has seen you drag your hand over your eyes to wipe away drops of sorrow, he has seen you place the hand on your heart, or press it against the hand of the ones that you loved. And so, while you feel the gentle rustle of your creature that you keep, you still stay asleep, but now you sleep with the attitude of a person who is about to walk into a surprise party that you are guessing might be there and that you really wanted, because it proves that your friends love you.

You feel the force of love pulling you into the day and you keep your eyes closed.

You could maybe float out of the bed. Your palm is open.

The dog presses a small, dry black paw into your open hand and the curtain between the dreaming and waking worlds blows away and the day is opening to you and you are invited in by one of your dearest companions. And you, you sweetheart, you good creature, one of your dearest companions is this old animal.

And he has said nothing, just this gesture: Paw to palm, on purpose.

He has spoken the most important thing, which is "Here we are again in a new day. I want you to see it with me." And this description above is an example of how you can gaze on yourself with love when nobody is there to do that for you, and how you can make it so that your own loving gaze is truthful and not obsessive or vain. You can wake up like this, be this, and tell yourself that this is an example of how a day can start on Earth.

Blue Hour

At the end of the summer, after many returns of waking up in safe, muggy gray mornings by the Atlantic, after a brief trip to New York City during which I get my picture taken a lot, feel both gorgeous and also that there is no place or life for me in that city anymore, after I go back to a Massachusetts so heavy with heat and an orchestral din of nighttime bugs, skunks under the porch, old people coming out of the woodwork to say, "There is a whole group of sisters on the Hurwitz side that you never met because of how your great-grandmother died in the fire," after my sister gets married in a darling and pure dash of light, I spend two days eating leftovers, feel a heavy heat in my body, and leave.

But right before I left, it was the wedding.

I spent the wedding weekend with couples. I was not sorry for myself. I was just fine. I was more disturbed that it seems impossible to me that I will ever find someone for myself after all of this. I am bitter sometimes. I think, "Why should I have to sleep alone? What is wrong with me? What happened to my allure, which in my last decade seemed almost problematic?"

And during the wedding, I was working on forgetting the past, letting myself only have the buoyant and real glee that was the soul of the event. But it was harder to hang on to my newfound knowledge of contentment with solitude. The jostling and interrupting was occurring. I put my own habit of fretting over myself on hold. I let myself be a drifting wisp in the wedding.

A young man said, *Hello, are you the sister of the bride?*

Yes, I am the older sister but not the oldest sister and I am the middle daughter and I am here by myself. And then the conversation begins but it is very boring.

211

The reason I think that it will be hard to meet someone who I am actually interested in is that I cannot stand
these preliminary moments when you can't deeply know
each other and be together forever. My ex-husband says
to me on the phone, after I tell him that I am lonely and
I think I am weird around men, that I am not weird but
that I am trying to force an intimacy that needs time to
grow. He is right and he knows me very well.

The other problem is that lots of people are simply not
the right fit, but somehow I always make it my fault, even
though it is nobody's fault at all when you don't fit.

This man here now is talking to me about something
about computers and I just can't listen well because I
don't like computers. I could never love him. There is no
way of getting around it. I can imagine him drinking apple juice and eating graham crackers and having crumbs
on his wet mouth, drinking that juice that is the color of
pee-pee. Not a good sign.

He is telling me something that I don't care about.
The next thing that happens *is* something I care about:
My deep-self jumps in to protect me from being bored
and starts to tell me something that kind of slides over
what he is saying. I make sure to provide a *listening face*
for the talking fellow and then I let myself listen to the
voice inside of me.

My deep-self asks, "Would you like to hear something that is useful to you?"

Yes. But aren't I doing the thing that I'm supposed to stop doing? That thing where I am either forcing the intimacy or completely ignoring somebody?

"You only force intimacy because you have a hungry heart and you have been displaced. It's a condition of the heart, based on your situation. You are looking for a place in another."

I'm tired of looking for a place in another.

"I know. That's why I'm here. I found the place where you're supposed to be. I figured it out. And it leads to all the other places you will ever want to go."

Great. This man is still talking about his trip to South America. I think I can hold the listening face a little longer. Can you make it brief?

"Unlikely! (I'm from you.)"

Okay, go! I will stick my finger in the cake while this man talks, I guess.

"Why do you have to stay here pretending to listen to him?"

Good point. I just walked away from the man, saying that I have to use the bathroom, but of course I am going toward the bar. I'm going to drink wine and watch my grandmothers as they sit or dance.

"I'd really like your undivided attention. You've never given it to me before."

I haven't? Who exactly are you, in me? Are you my date to this wedding?

"I'm you, you know that, don't be a smartass just because you are drunk. Maybe now is not the best time."

Okay. But I'm glad you're here. And will you not give up very easily, please?

"No. I will not give up. I'm here to remind you that there is much more than this one moment of being uncomfortable. We'll talk tomorrow."

I woke up the day after the wedding and I was in a state of contentment. I had breakfast in a clean dress, by myself in the hotel. I wasn't thinking about *alone and fine with that* versus *alone and devastated.* I was working on new terms with my deep-self.

I scanned the newspaper and I said, "Okay, let's get a new plan together. Do you have thoughts?"

"Yes. I've put together a little list of oaths and goals. If you live by them, you will clear a path to the place for you."

Great, let it rip.

"Okay, first: You will wear all monochromatic outfits."

Oh, damn. This is what I've been waiting for.

"You will have hardly any plastic in your house."

Yes, I get it. Go on and I won't interrupt but just know that I. Am. In.

"I know you are. More now: You will not turn on the TV very much. You will take the houseplants seriously, very seriously, maybe even researching how to fix things like mold or gnats in the soil.

"You will cook yourself meals and stop doing that thing where you wait until it is the time in the evening when you are both hungry and lonely and end up getting some huge soup delivered and then splatter yourself with it.

"You will really let the dog know that he is your companion and you are his."

Yes. I know you. I just want to interrupt to say that I forgot you and I'm sorry but I do know you.

"It's fine. Listen now: You will be cleaned by your own focus, by not being seduced into self-indulgence. You will become a peaceful authority who says no to that voice that wants to undermine and splash you with the gloop of self-doubt in an effort to stall your emergence.

"You will tell yourself that good, gentle civility and loving self-discipline are essential.

"You will not be exhausted anymore by the fight with the misogynist in your psyche. You will remember that the misogynist in your head is peddling propaganda that has been written in your own blood, forged in the fires of your own personal hell. You will admit that this has been a very big problem for you."

Oh my goodness.

"You won't let the idiots and the assholes get past the front gate of your heart. They can yell from the sidewalk. They can yell terrible things, because they are shut out and can't stand to be let go, but you will not let them in now."

Oh, damn. Yes.

"Repeat this in your head: There are no odds to beat anymore, just some real junk to dump. You dump your junk. After you dump it, you don't sort it in your mind. You dump your junk and you walk away. You wear all one color on the outside, swirl with every color on the inside. You walk forward. You keep your head angled up so that you see over the fray. You protect yourself and all the little weirds that make up who you are."

We sat there and had the coffee and eggs in the in-between world, the often scary but necessary space between old patterns and new behaviors. I didn't know it then, but I'd made it to the holy land.

I can't remember the plane ride home, but if I'd been cheering in the sky, that wouldn't sound like gossip to me. It would sound like a reasonable report.

* * *

And now it is now, which is the future. I have been living with myself. I have been living by the new creed. I'm trying to say what changed. I was at the end of a long wander, of a long time of separation. I thought the separation was one from other people, but of course, the call was coming from inside the house, as they say.

I write this in a small room in my home, during the time of the morning when it is cool and blue. Everything is a variation of eucalyptus. Outside, the air is blue and the leaves are types of blues and the chill in the air is a good blue as well. I am running cool too.

There is no sun up but it is not night anymore. It is the in-between time that most people say is just for animals to wake up in, the space between day and night when ghosts have to go back to the flat realm where they file away like love letters, apologies, curses.

I am awake in the blue hour and I sit on a chair in a nightgown and just out of view, a ghost is whirled away and replaced with a lizard that creaks up an eyelid by my garage.

No stores or restaurants are open yet, although I am sure there are people baking already, in the places where the other people will go inside, hungry and wearing their T-shirts, with their babies, with their loves. I am here, in

217

this time of the morning when nobody is apparent but myself. I now look so forward to this time before the world is on. I wake up and I am tired but once my feet hit the ground and I know that it is still very early, I feel relief.

The kettle waits for me. I open all the old windows. I am a young woman still. I have cropped my hair to my jaw. I am not taking any more nonsense.

Outside now everything is shifting shades as the day sweeps in. The first thing to go from blue to green is the grapefruit tree. Then from blue to fuchsia are the bougainvillea, then from blood blue to juice red are the geraniums that I require. They fill boxes. They make a fringe of fire around my house. The peppermint geranium, which is only big furry leaves (no blooms, only scent), switches from blue pads to green-gray fans of fauna.

My small tidy breathing, soft thighs on the chair, my hands touching each other, my eyes open and steady, my life.

It was not necessarily a choice at the outset, but now it is certainly a point of pride that I functionally dwell in realms that I was once afraid of. The darks and the in-betweens. They all fortify me. I am a citizen of many dimensions, and now I slip between them easily. I never slip away from myself by simplifying myself. I can't become smaller to fit into a crouching love in somebody else's meager world.

I don't do that anymore. I have calmed down. I have consolidated. I have come through the reckoning that I required.

I have crept into this blue hour so gingerly as to not disturb it or bounce the sun up into the sky. I can travel from an early-morning world of still blues into the clip-clop of this green daytime regalia without seeming like I stayed too long at the dark party and now I am in the day by mistake. There is a time of the day when there is no light, did you know that? I never let myself know that before, but now I know it and I face the day when it is still dark. I face the darkness with the faith in the light, without any rush. I shift and slide with the time as it flows forward. I am not a wandering spirit, I am a walking woman. I have a place in the shifts. I don't have to wrangle intimacy anymore, because I am engaging with it constantly, with the intimacy within, so that I can be a part of this chill flux.

I didn't feel like this before, when I was more scared, but now I wake up when the dead are walking their last loops and the newest drops of dew are pouting on the persimmons. I don't have to wait to be here anymore. An animal like me lives all the time, everywhere. I didn't feel it before but now I do.

All of these times, the hours where you can't see anything and the ones where you can see your whole form, and all of the ways that the shapes and shadows fall in between, these are all hours during which I have given myself permission to keep time. I am that mysterious stranger that I hoped to meet. I met her at a dark dance. We came here to live together until I could stay by myself.

The place is here. The time is now. This is all my lifetime.

From me to you, from me to everybody

I look up to you because I love the heavenly bodies of the universe, and the way I see it, your heart is a planet.

Your heart is factually a part of the universe, which is a miracle of endless force and boundless beauty.

There is literally no way that you are not part of that.

Despair can force you to turn your eyes away from this fact, but it is the real truth and it will be waiting to be with you when you are free enough to turn back to it.

Your heart is a planet. I can see that you are from the sky.

Acknowledgments

Thank you to the people who encouraged me, assisted me, bolstered me, listened to me even though that must have been very irritating at times, loved me, hired me, fired me, took me in, and let me go. Thank you to Ron Slate, my father, who sat with me and read everything. Thank you to Nancy Slate, who receives my teary phone calls from the other side of the country, who took me straight from the airport to the alpaca farm when I asked her to, no questions asked. Thank you to my sisters, Abby Ciampa and Stacey Slate, for saving my life many times, for being the kindest women I will ever know. Thank you to Mike Ciampa and Johannes Epke for being my real friends and dream brothers. Thank you to my grandparents, Lester Gilson, Connie

Gilson, Rochelle Slate, and Paul Slate, for giving me so much joy and an education and many Barbies and potato chips and Jell-O. Thank you to Barbara, Rich, Emma, and Anna Rollins for walks in the woods and many good meals. Thank you to my friends, who have never once shut me out or shamed me, and who I will love forever: Quinn Lundberg, Zach Galifianakis, Gabe Liedman, Daniel Zomparelli, Lang Fisher, Sarah Taylor, Nellie Killian, Mike Barry, Grey Brooks, Max Silvestri, Leah Beckmann, Mae Whitman, Jane Levy, Mallory Wedding, Dean Fleischer-Camp, Gillian Robespierre, Elisabeth Holm, Jennifer Schwartz, Anne Nicholson, and all of the Camp Tapawingo Girls. Thank you to Rebecca Dinerstein and John Knight for caring for me and having fun with me all over this globe, for endless encouragement, patience and tiny wooden animals. Thank you to Claudia Ballard for her endless support, and to Jean Garnett for her guidance and kindness and incredible skills as an editor and general human being. And to Ben Shattuck, the person who I might thank forever, for so much. Thank you for letting me be wild, and for giving me a home in your heart. Superlatives are dangerous, but I'll put it in writing: You are the best sweetheart, a dream love, a true weirdo, and the biggest and best surprise of my life.